The prince in his dark days

Hico Yamanaka

2

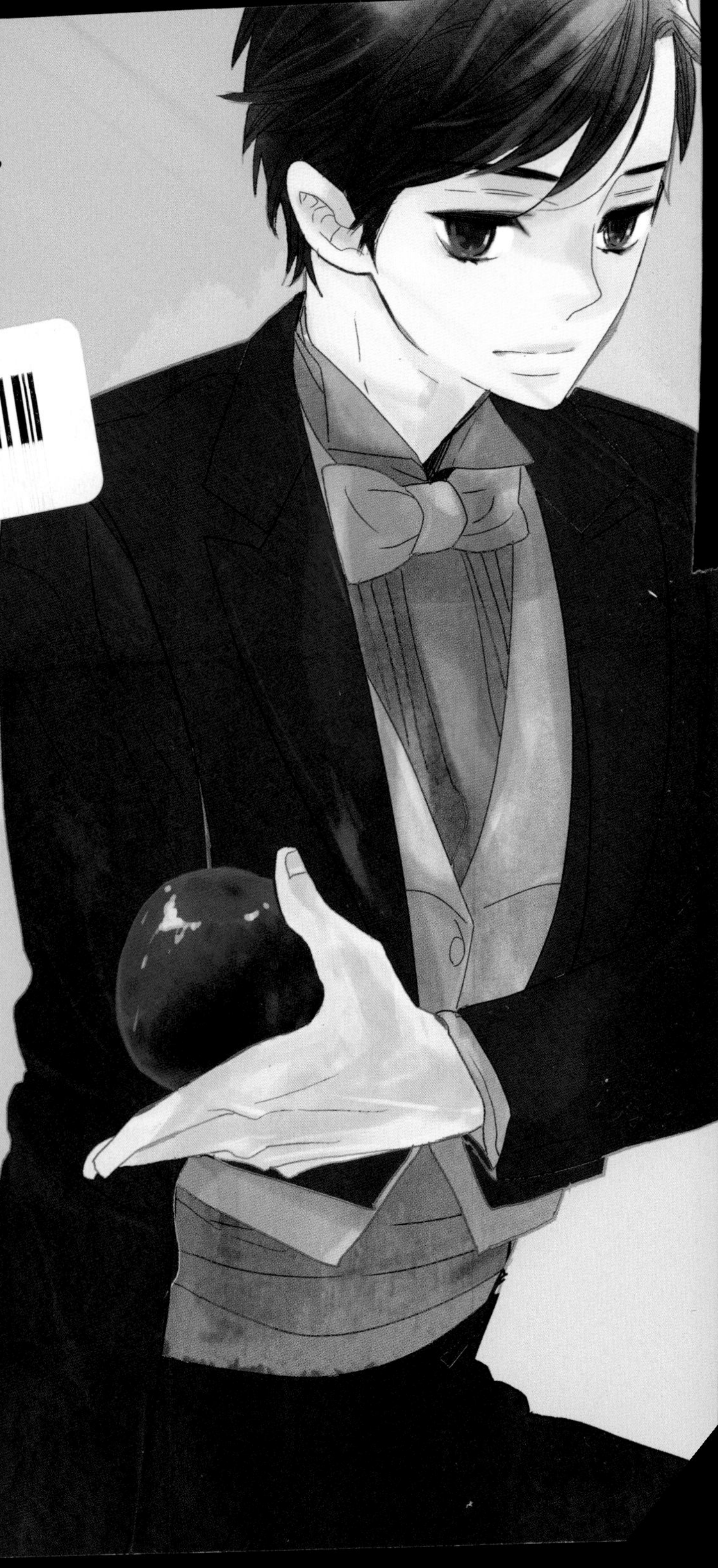

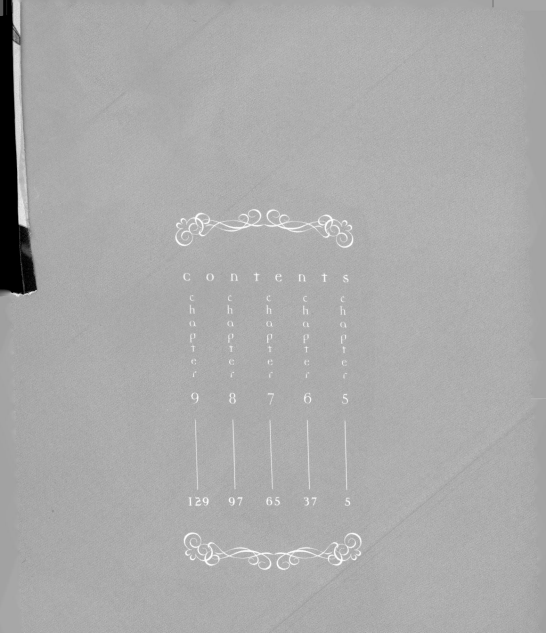

contents

The prince in his Dark Days

Hico Yamanaka

character

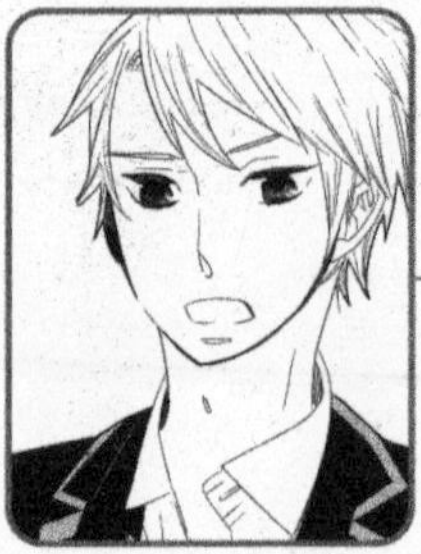

The stand-in.

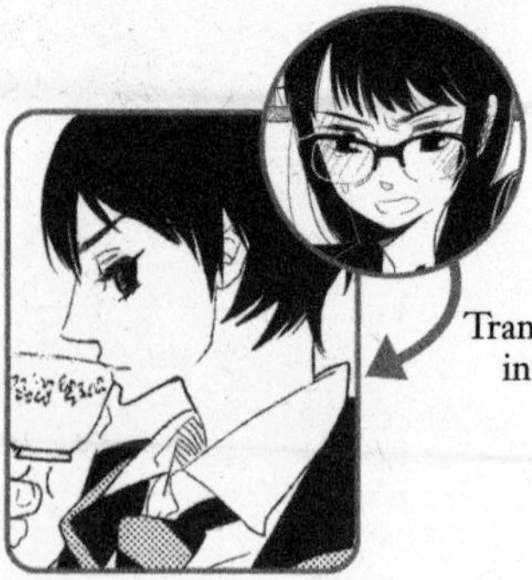

Transforms into...

Itaru Nogi

Heir to a wealthy family.
His hobby of dressing in women's clothing is a dire secret. Fed up with the restraints of his princely lifestyle, he runs away.

Atsuko Ôkawa

A high school girl born into a poor household. She looks just like Itaru, so she is dressing as a man and acting as his double.

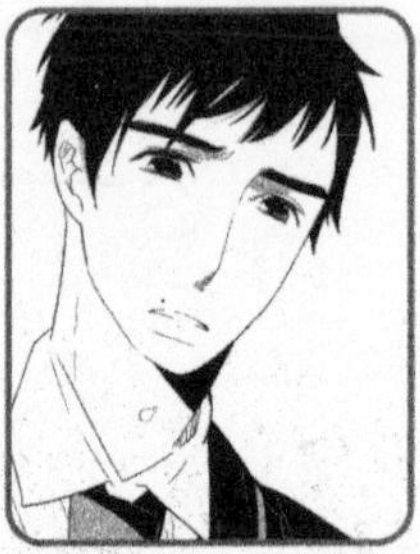

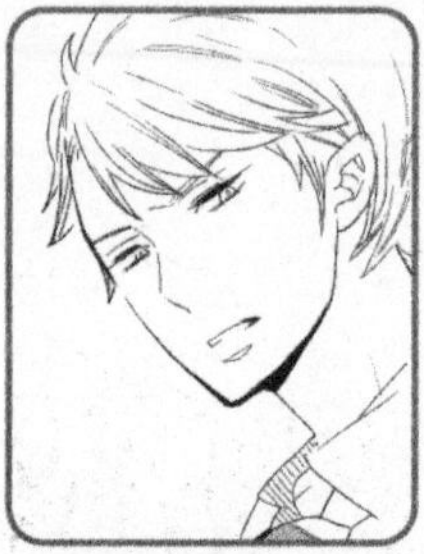

Nobunari Mukai

A longtime friend of Itaru and Ryô.
He is in love with Itaru.

Ryô Sekiuchi

Itaru's half-brother.
After Itaru's disappearance, he trains Atsuko and accompanies her everywhere.

story

Atsuko is a high school girl living a miserable life of poverty. One day, she meets Itaru—the heir to the Nogi Group—and his right-hand men, Ryô and Nobunari. Atsuko's fate changes when Itaru, the wealthy heir who looks just like her, suddenly disappears. She begins to dress as a man and live in a palatial estate as Itaru's double. Despite her rigorous training and her heartbreak over Nobunari, the joy of being needed inspires Atsuko to continue her efforts to be the perfect prince. But palace life isn't as charmed as she had believed—she discovers complicated relationships between the prince and his associates, and the suffering that comes with them...

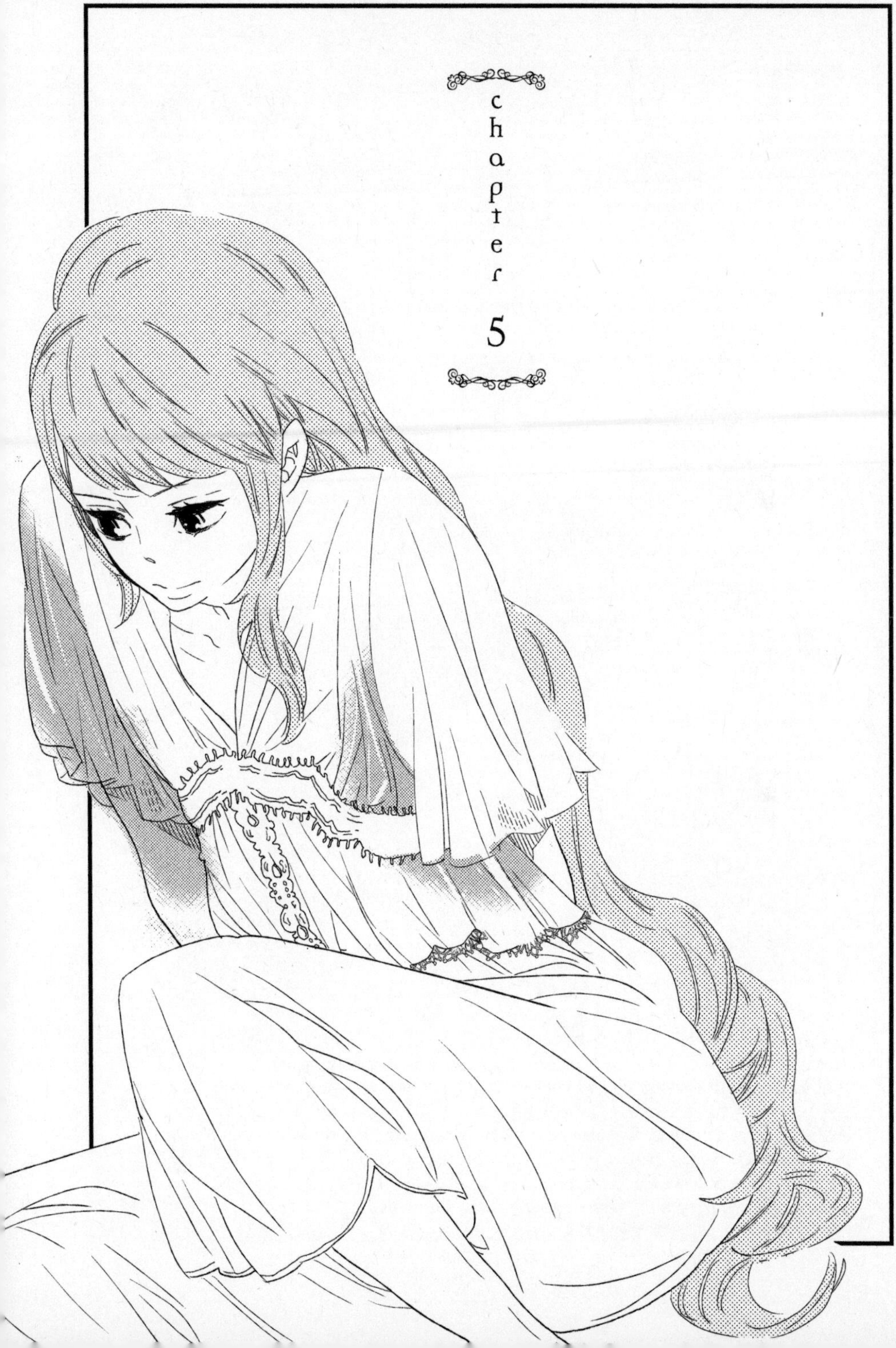
chapter
5

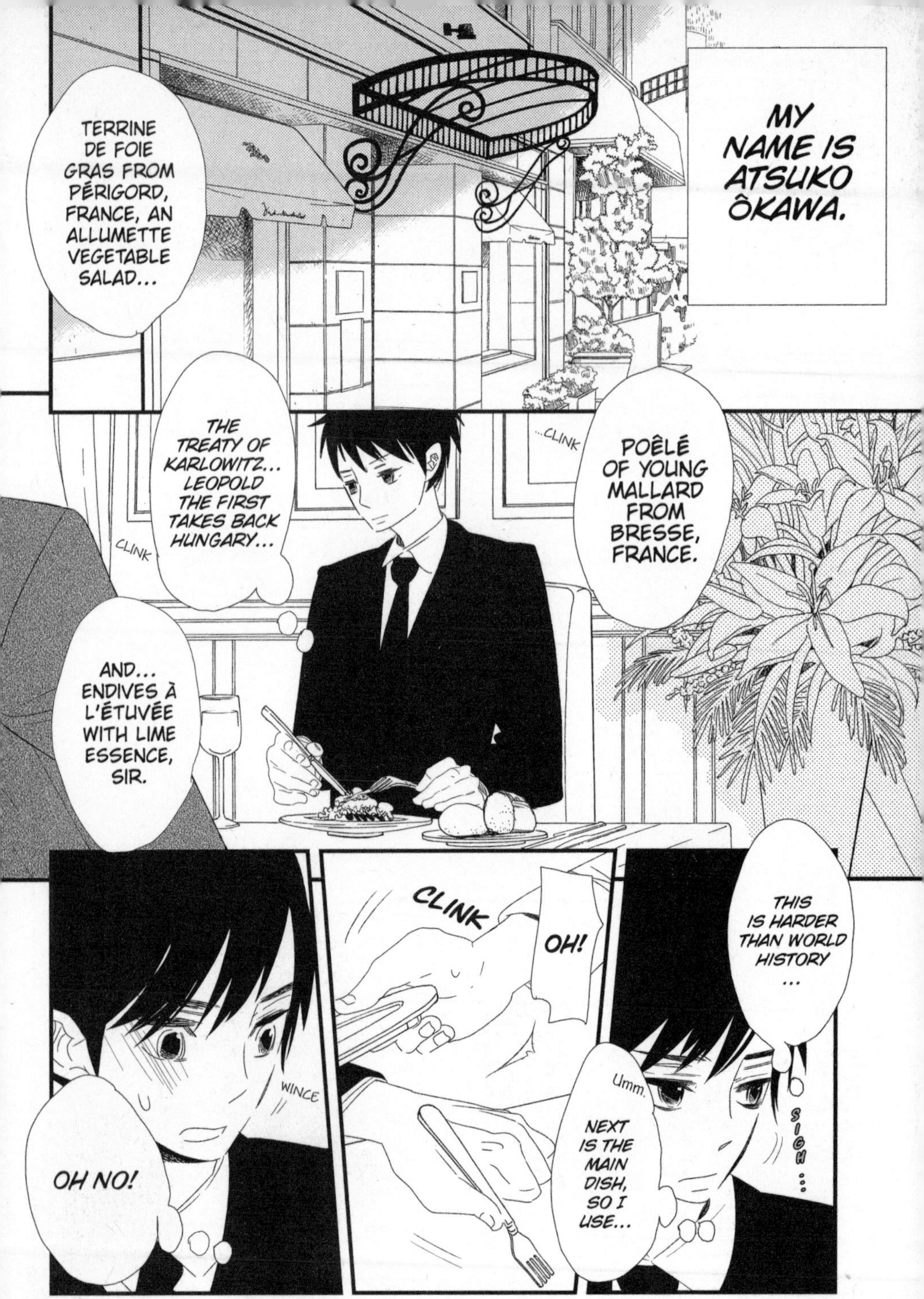

MY NAME IS ATSUKO ÔKAWA.
TERRINE DE FOIE GRAS FROM PÉRIGORD, FRANCE, AN ALLUMETTE VEGETABLE SALAD...
POÊLÉ OF YOUNG MALLARD FROM BRESSE, FRANCE.
...CLINK
THE TREATY OF KARLOWITZ... LEOPOLD THE FIRST TAKES BACK HUNGARY...
CLINK
AND... ENDIVES À L'ÉTUVÉE WITH LIME ESSENCE, SIR.
THIS IS HARDER THAN WORLD HISTORY ...
SIGH ...
Umm.
NEXT IS THE MAIN DISH, SO I USE...
CLINK
OH!
WINCE
OH NO!

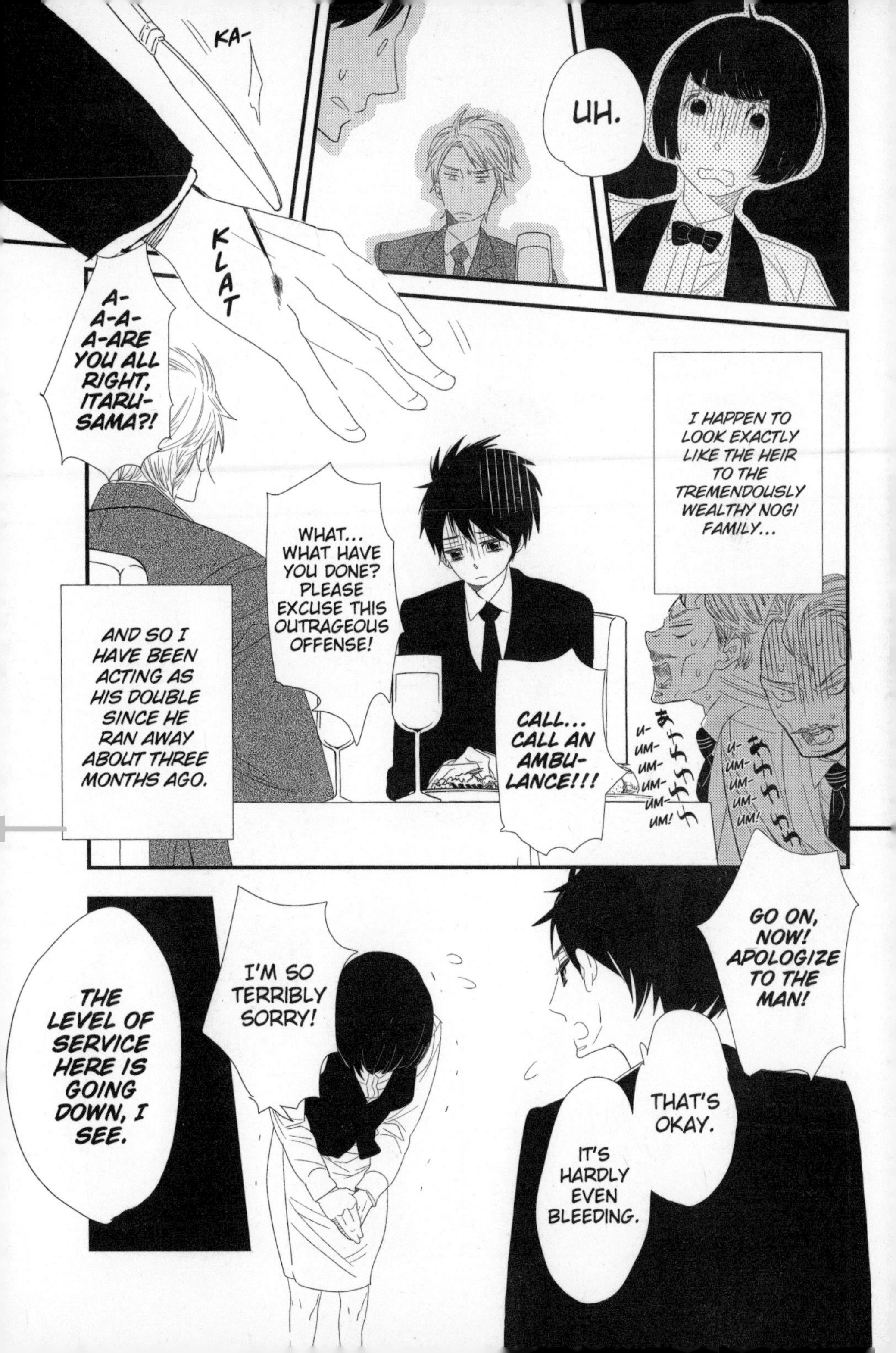
UH.
KA-
KLAT
I HAPPEN TO LOOK EXACTLY LIKE THE HEIR TO THE TREMENDOUSLY WEALTHY NOGI FAMILY...
A-A-A-A-ARE YOU ALL RIGHT, ITARU-SAMA?!
WHAT... WHAT HAVE YOU DONE? PLEASE EXCUSE THIS OUTRAGEOUS OFFENSE!
U-UM-UM-UM-UM!
U-UM-UM-UM-UM!
CALL... CALL AN AMBULANCE!!!
AND SO I HAVE BEEN ACTING AS HIS DOUBLE SINCE HE RAN AWAY ABOUT THREE MONTHS AGO.
GO ON, NOW! APOLOGIZE TO THE MAN!
THAT'S OKAY.
IT'S HARDLY EVEN BLEEDING.
I'M SO TERRIBLY SORRY!
THE LEVEL OF SERVICE HERE IS GOING DOWN, I SEE.

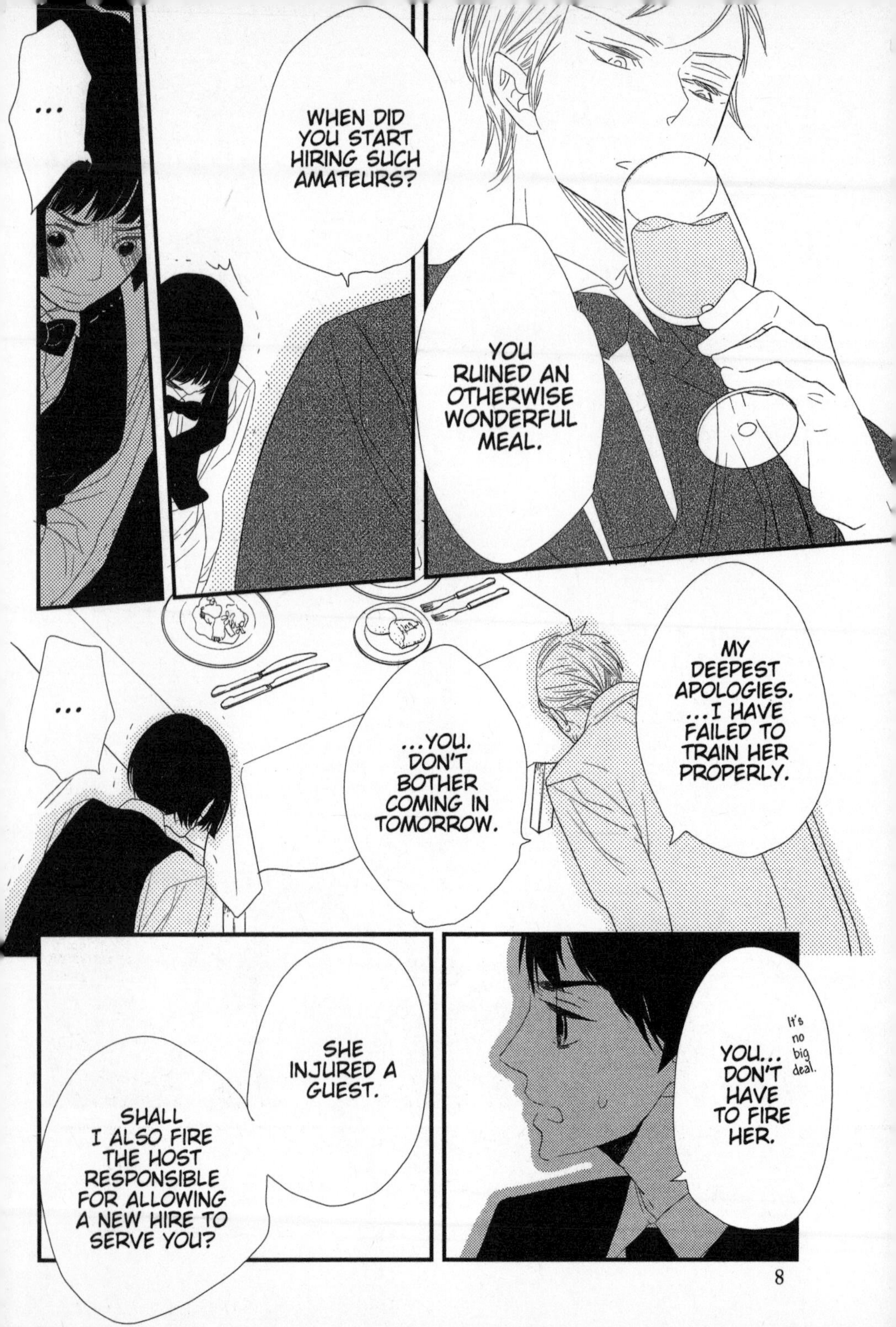
WHEN DID YOU START HIRING SUCH AMATEURS?
YOU RUINED AN OTHERWISE WONDERFUL MEAL.
...
MY DEEPEST APOLOGIES. ...I HAVE FAILED TO TRAIN HER PROPERLY.
...YOU. DON'T BOTHER COMING IN TOMORROW.
...
YOU... DON'T HAVE TO FIRE HER.
It's no big deal.
SHE INJURED A GUEST.
SHALL I ALSO FIRE THE HOST RESPONSIBLE FOR ALLOWING A NEW HIRE TO SERVE YOU?

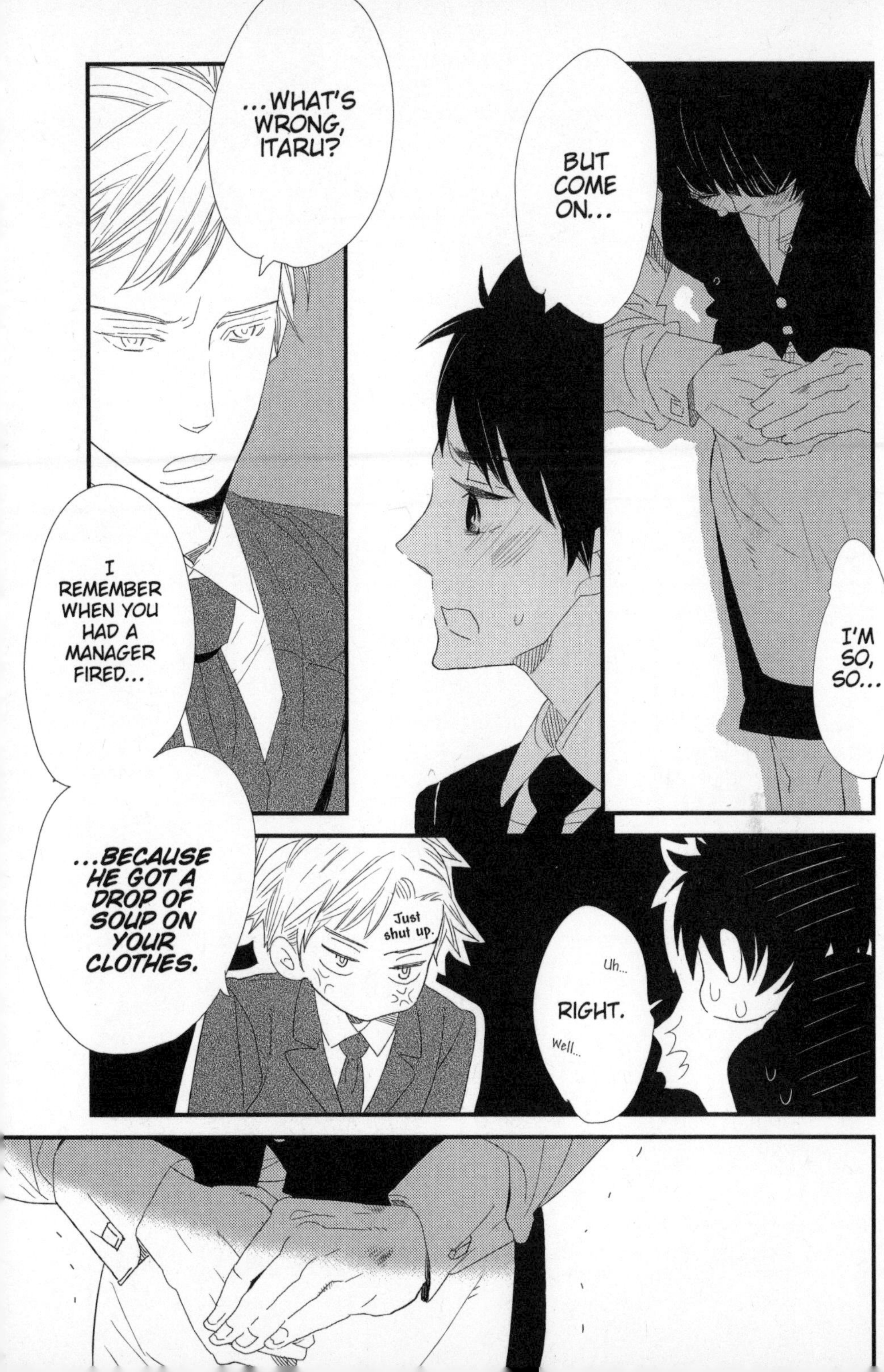
BUT COME ON...
I'M SO, SO...
...WHAT'S WRONG, ITARU?
I REMEMBER WHEN YOU HAD A MANAGER FIRED...
...BECAUSE HE GOT A DROP OF SOUP ON YOUR CLOTHES.
Uh...
RIGHT.
Well...
Just shut up.

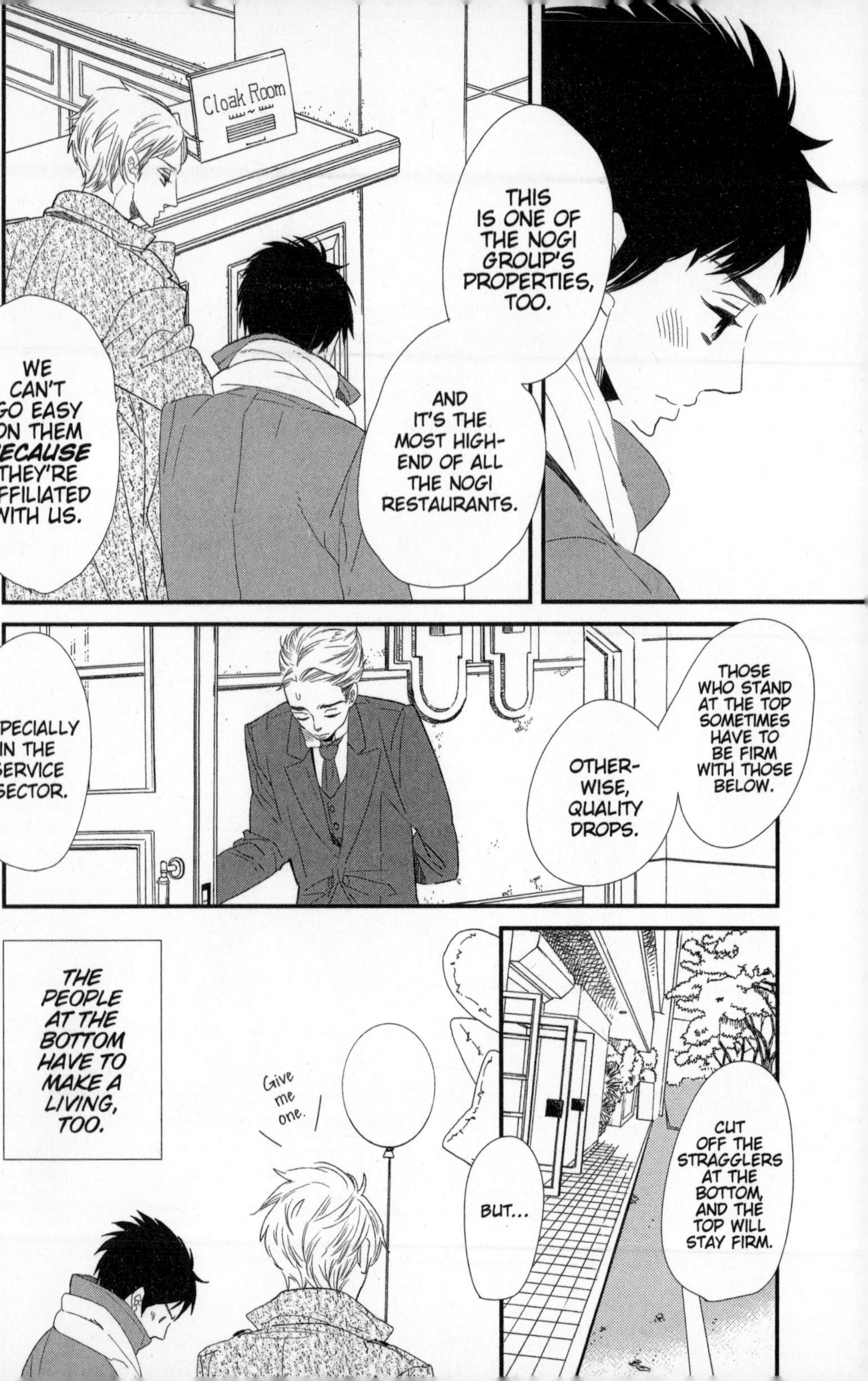
THIS IS ONE OF THE NOGI GROUP'S PROPERTIES, TOO.
AND IT'S THE MOST HIGH-END OF ALL THE NOGI RESTAURANTS.
Cloak Room
WE CAN'T GO EASY ON THEM *BECAUSE* THEY'RE AFFILIATED WITH US.
THOSE WHO STAND AT THE TOP SOMETIMES HAVE TO BE FIRM WITH THOSE BELOW.
OTHER-WISE, QUALITY DROPS.
ESPECIALLY IN THE SERVICE SECTOR.
CUT OFF THE STRAGGLERS AT THE BOTTOM, AND THE TOP WILL STAY FIRM.
BUT...
Give me one.
THE PEOPLE AT THE BOTTOM HAVE TO MAKE A LIVING, TOO.

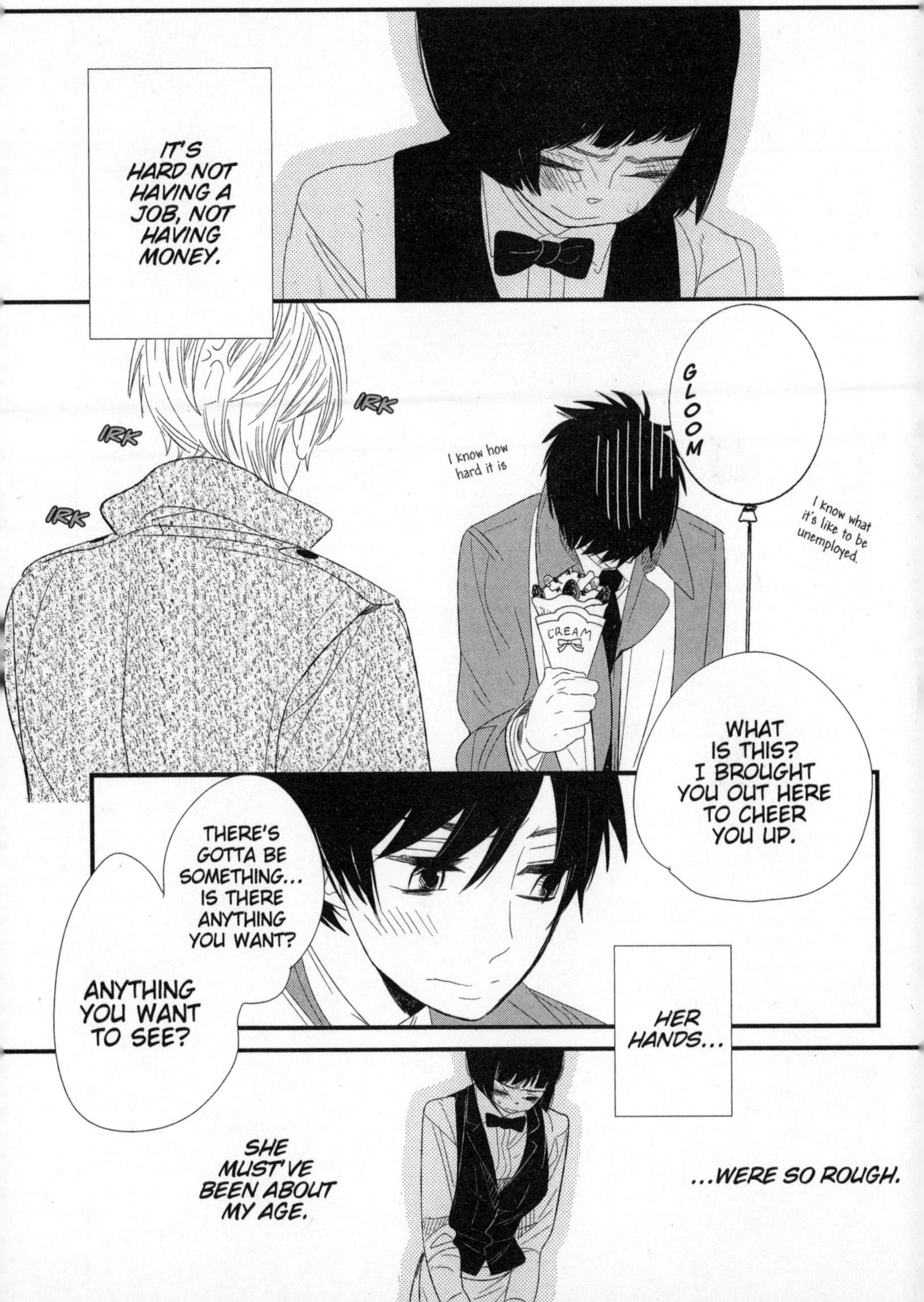
IT'S HARD NOT HAVING A JOB, NOT HAVING MONEY.
I know what it's like to be unemployed.
GLOOM
I know how hard it is
IRK
IRK
IRK
WHAT IS THIS? I BROUGHT YOU OUT HERE TO CHEER YOU UP.
CREAM
THERE'S GOTTA BE SOMETHING... IS THERE ANYTHING YOU WANT?
ANYTHING YOU WANT TO SEE?
HER HANDS...
...WERE SO ROUGH.
SHE MUST'VE BEEN ABOUT MY AGE.

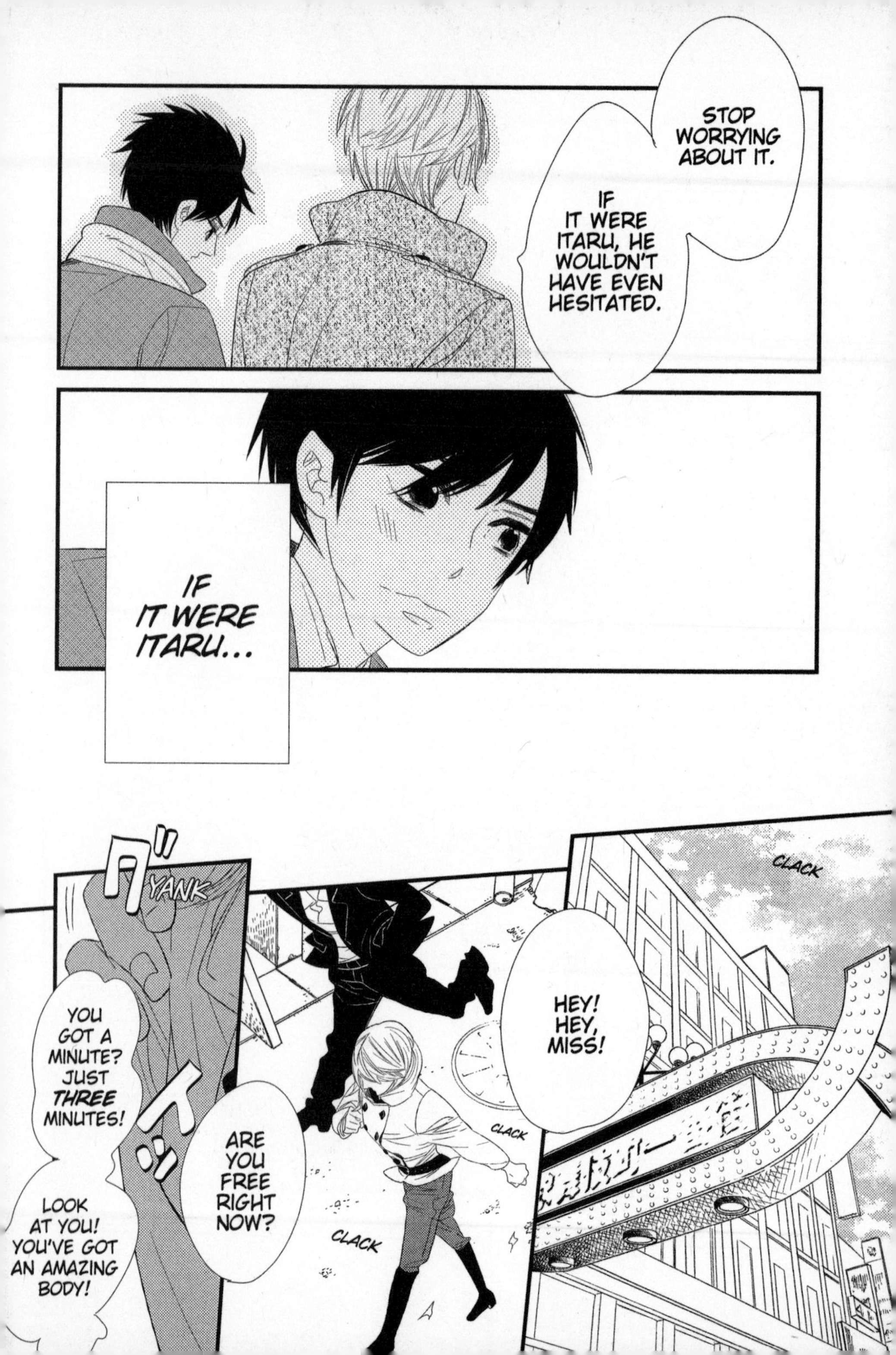
STOP WORRYING ABOUT IT.
IF IT WERE ITARU, HE WOULDN'T HAVE EVEN HESITATED.
IF IT WERE ITARU...
CLACK
HEY! HEY, MISS!
CLACK
ARE YOU FREE RIGHT NOW?
CLACK
YANK
YOU GOT A MINUTE? JUST THREE MINUTES!
LOOK AT YOU! YOU'VE GOT AN AMAZING BODY!

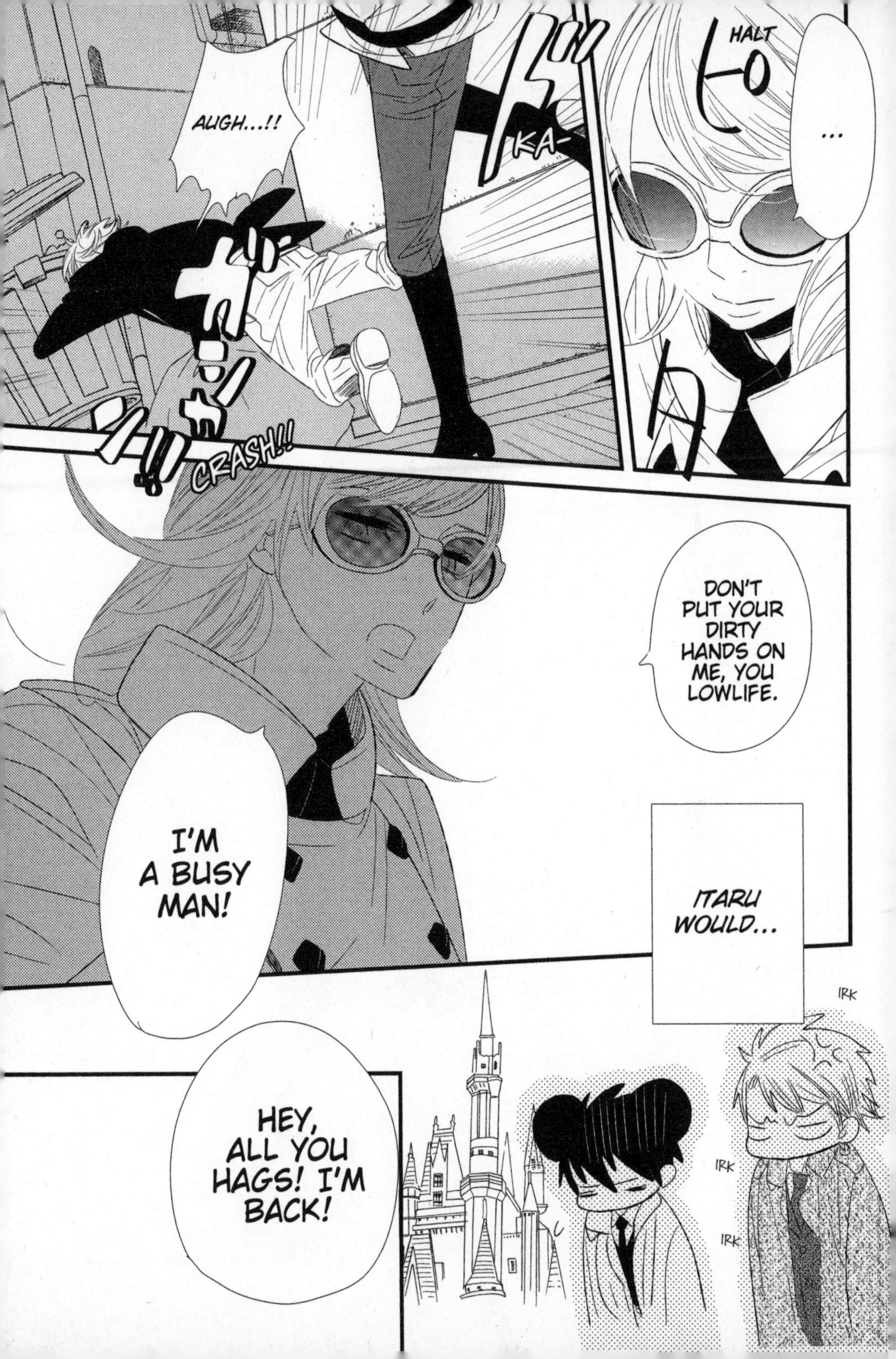
HALT
...
KA-
AUGH...!!
CRASH!!
DON'T PUT YOUR DIRTY HANDS ON ME, YOU LOWLIFE.
I'M A BUSY MAN!
ITARU WOULD...
IRK
IRK
IRK
HEY, ALL YOU HAGS! I'M BACK!

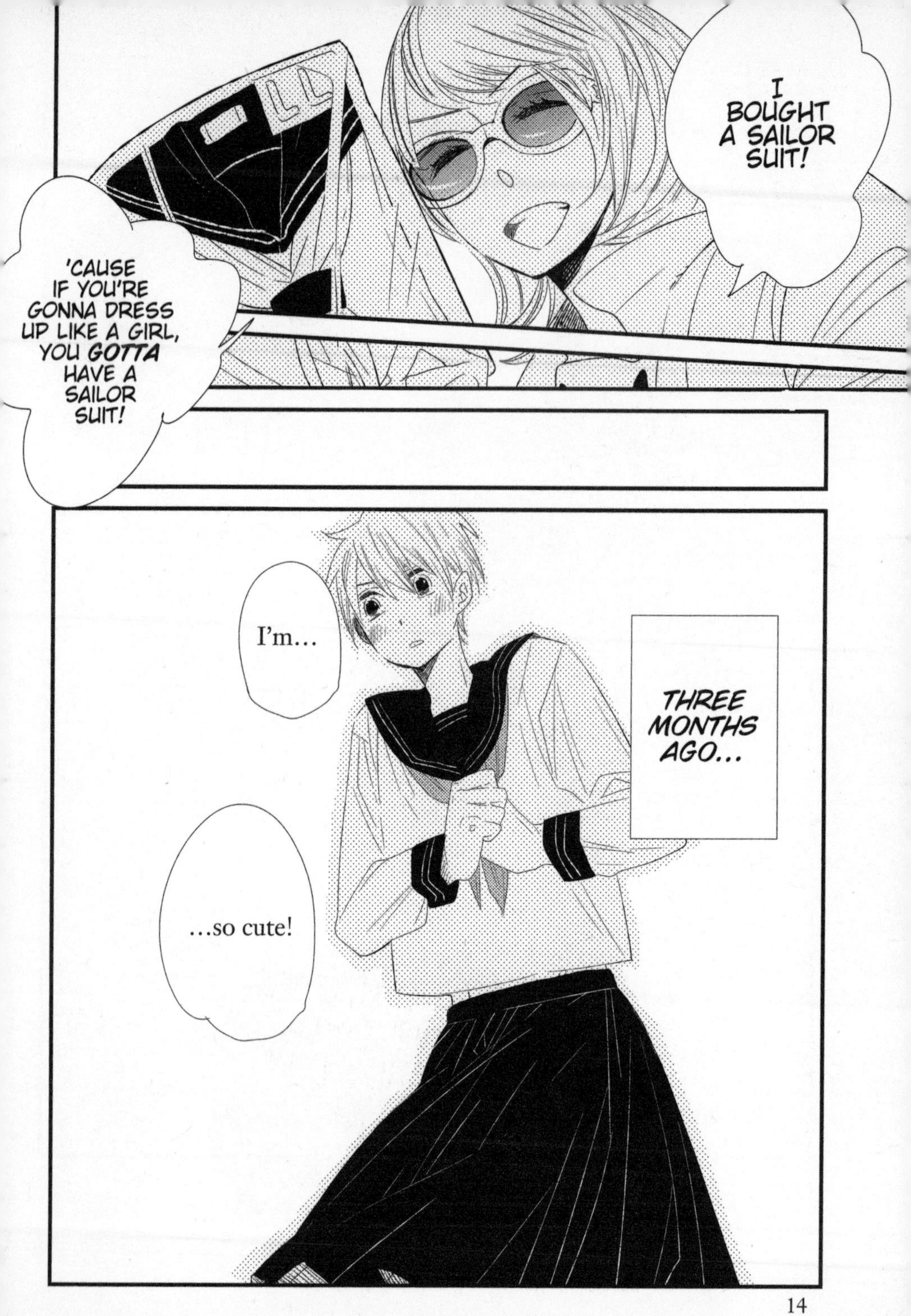
I BOUGHT A SAILOR SUIT!
'CAUSE IF YOU'RE GONNA DRESS UP LIKE A GIRL, YOU *GOTTA* HAVE A SAILOR SUIT!
THREE MONTHS AGO…
I'm…
…so cute!

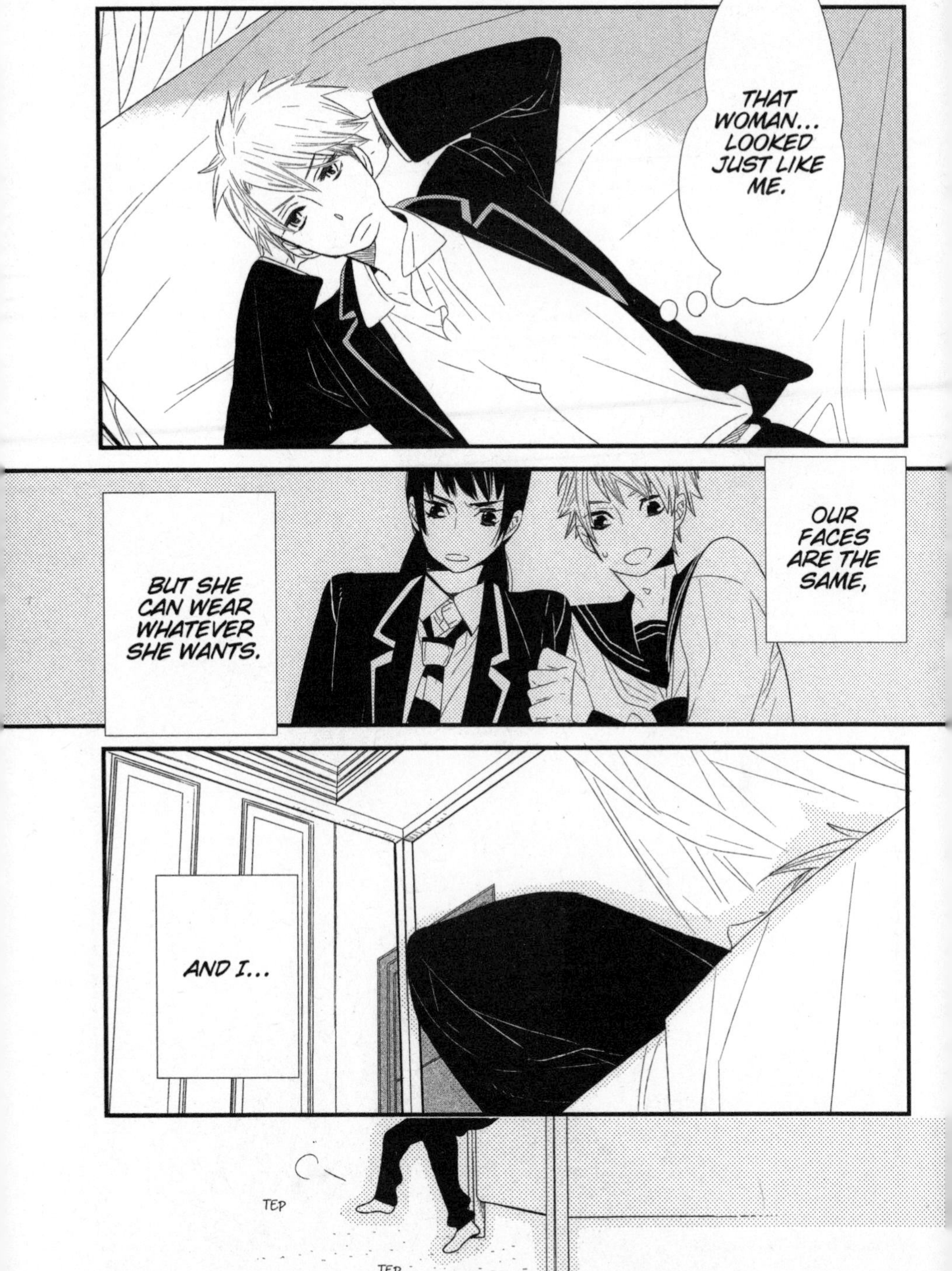
THAT WOMAN... LOOKED JUST LIKE ME.
OUR FACES ARE THE SAME,
BUT SHE CAN WEAR WHATEVER SHE WANTS.
AND I...
TEP
TEP

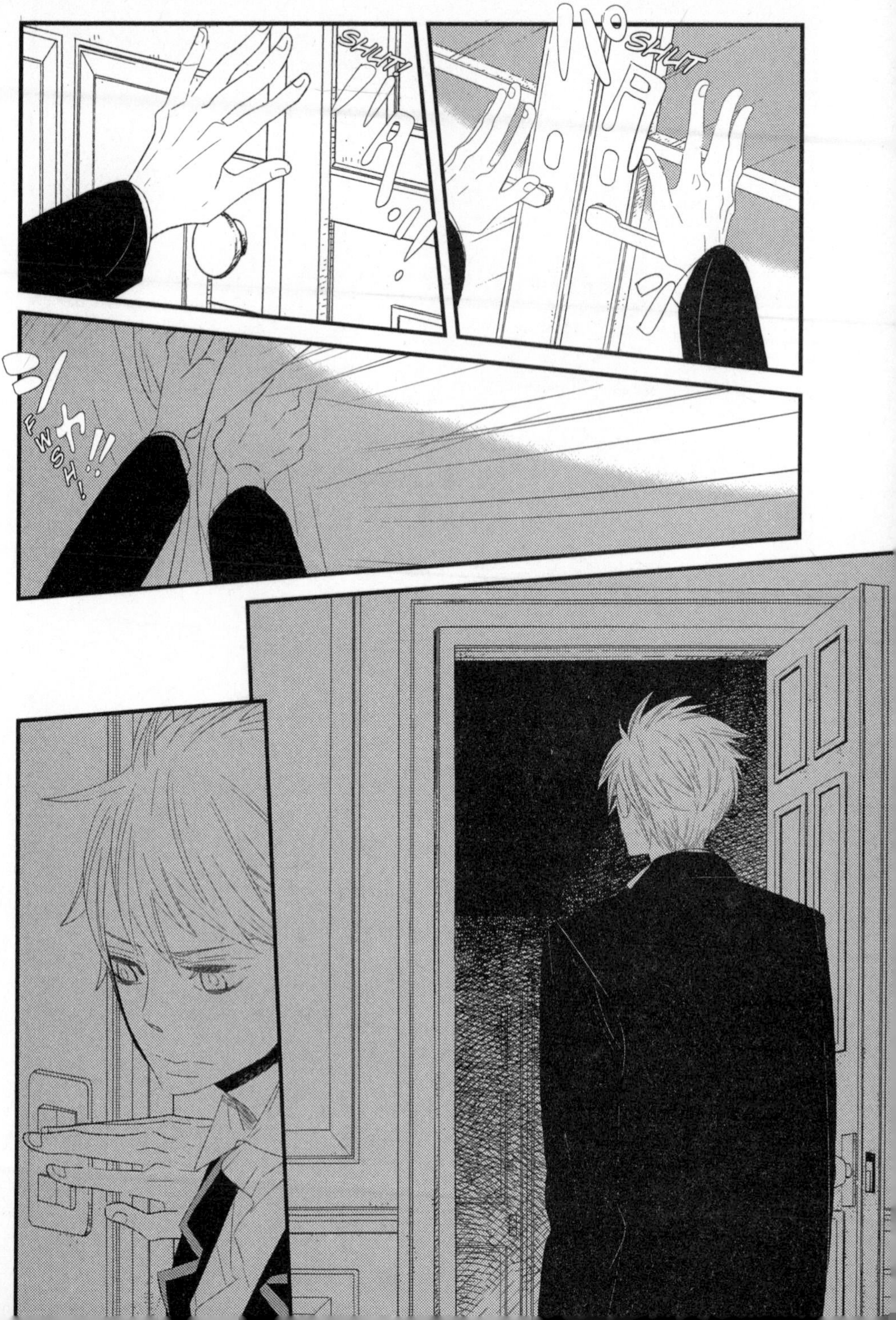
SHUT
SHUT!
FWSH!

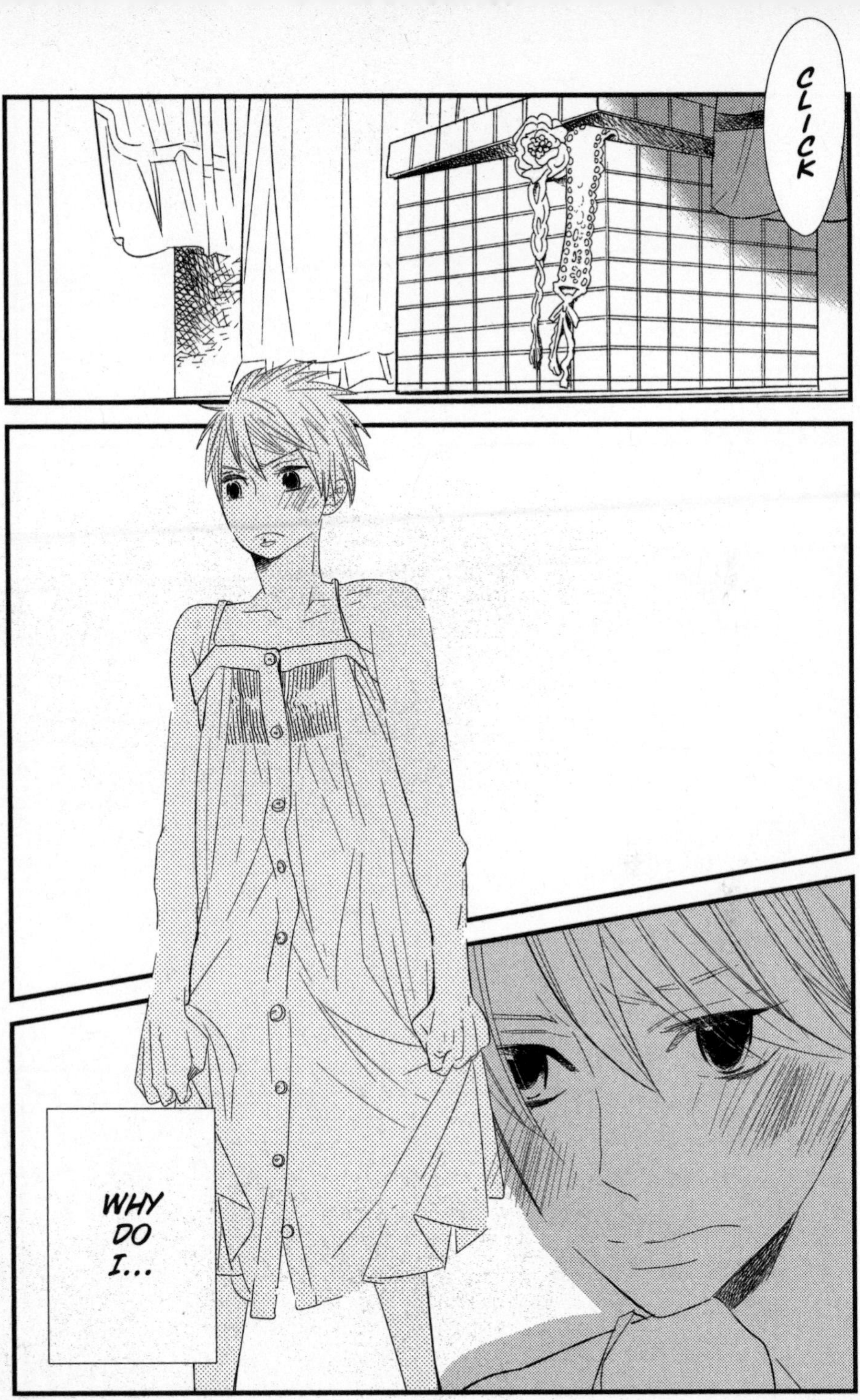
CLICK
WHY DO I...

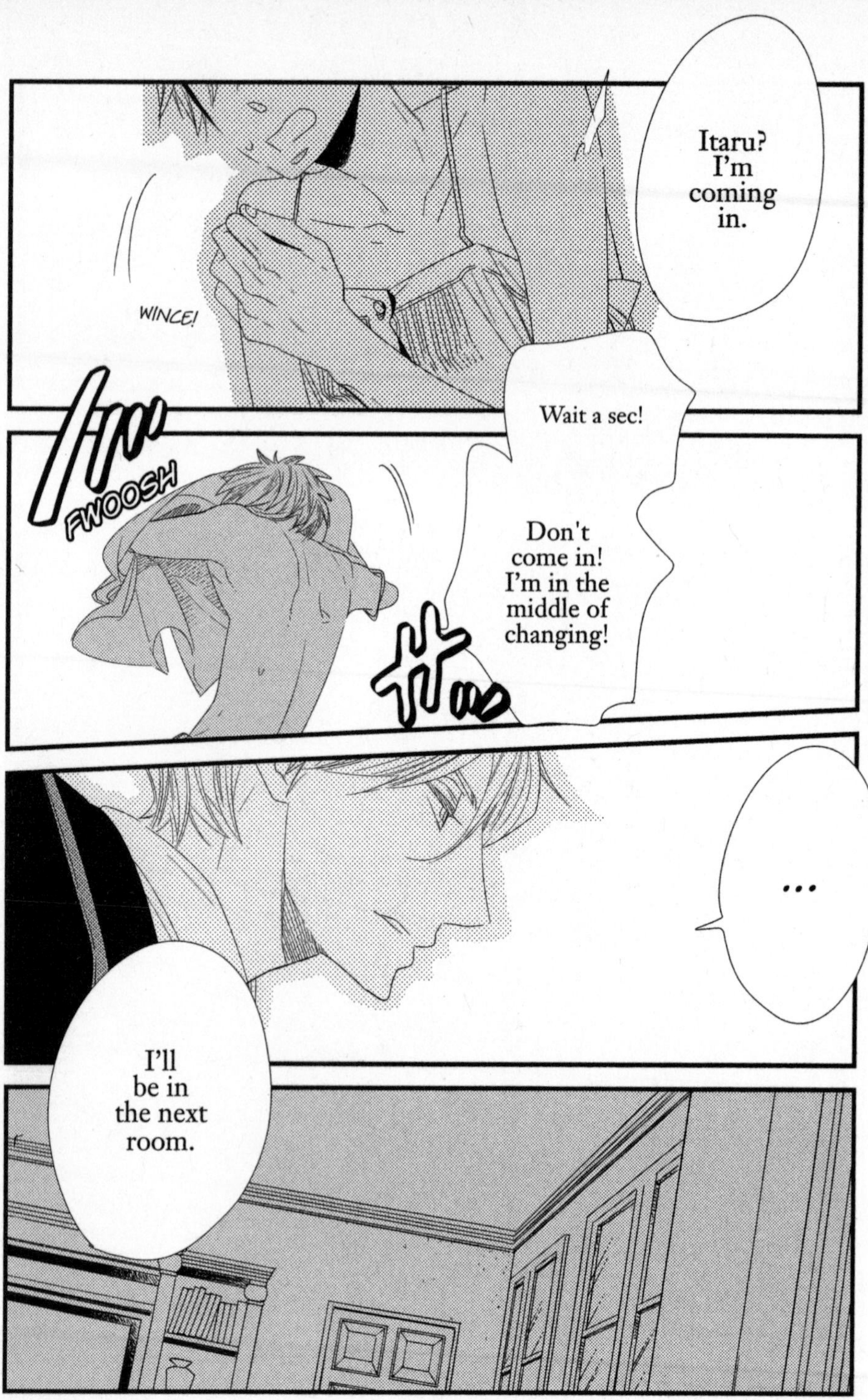

Itaru? I'm coming in.
WINCE!
Wait a sec!
Don't come in! I'm in the middle of changing!
FWOOSH
...
I'll be in the next room.

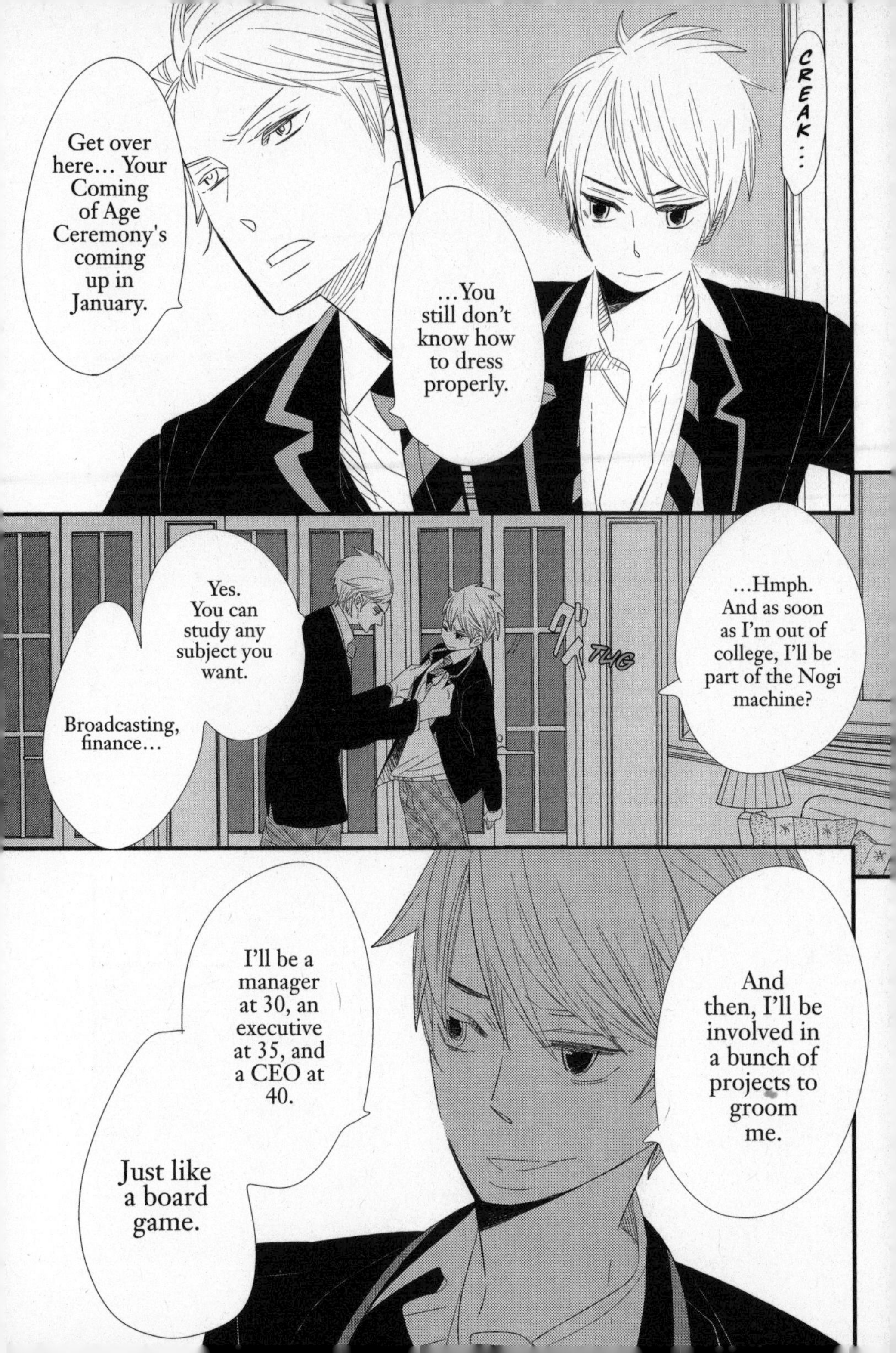
CREAK...
Get over here... Your Coming of Age Ceremony's coming up in January.
...You still don't know how to dress properly.
...Hmph. And as soon as I'm out of college, I'll be part of the Nogi machine?
TUG
Yes. You can study any subject you want.
Broadcasting, finance...
And then, I'll be involved in a bunch of projects to groom me.
I'll be a manager at 30, an executive at 35, and a CEO at 40.
Just like a board game.

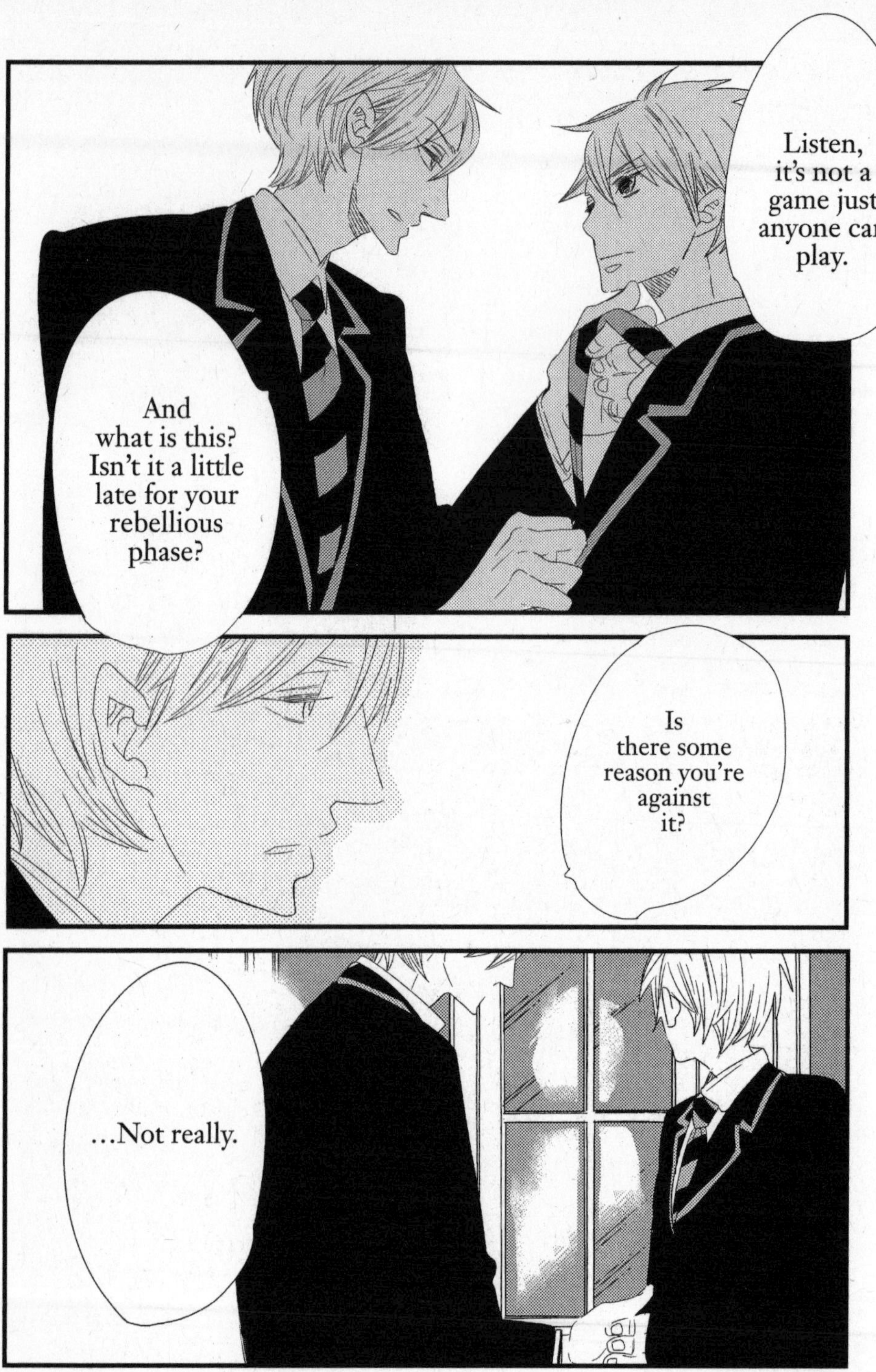
Listen, it's not a game just anyone can play.
And what is this? Isn't it a little late for your rebellious phase?
Is there some reason you're against it?
...Not really.

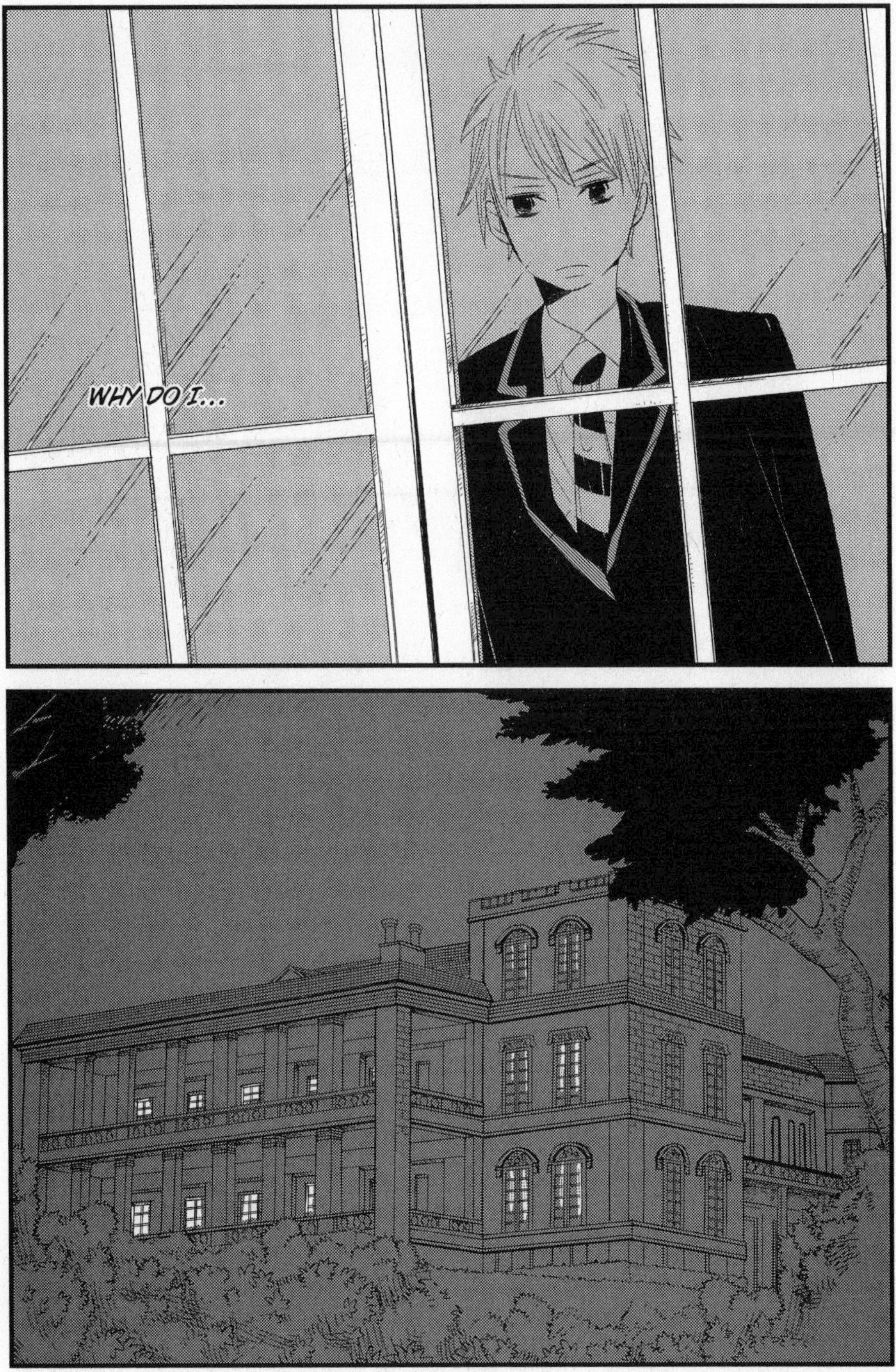
WHY DO I...

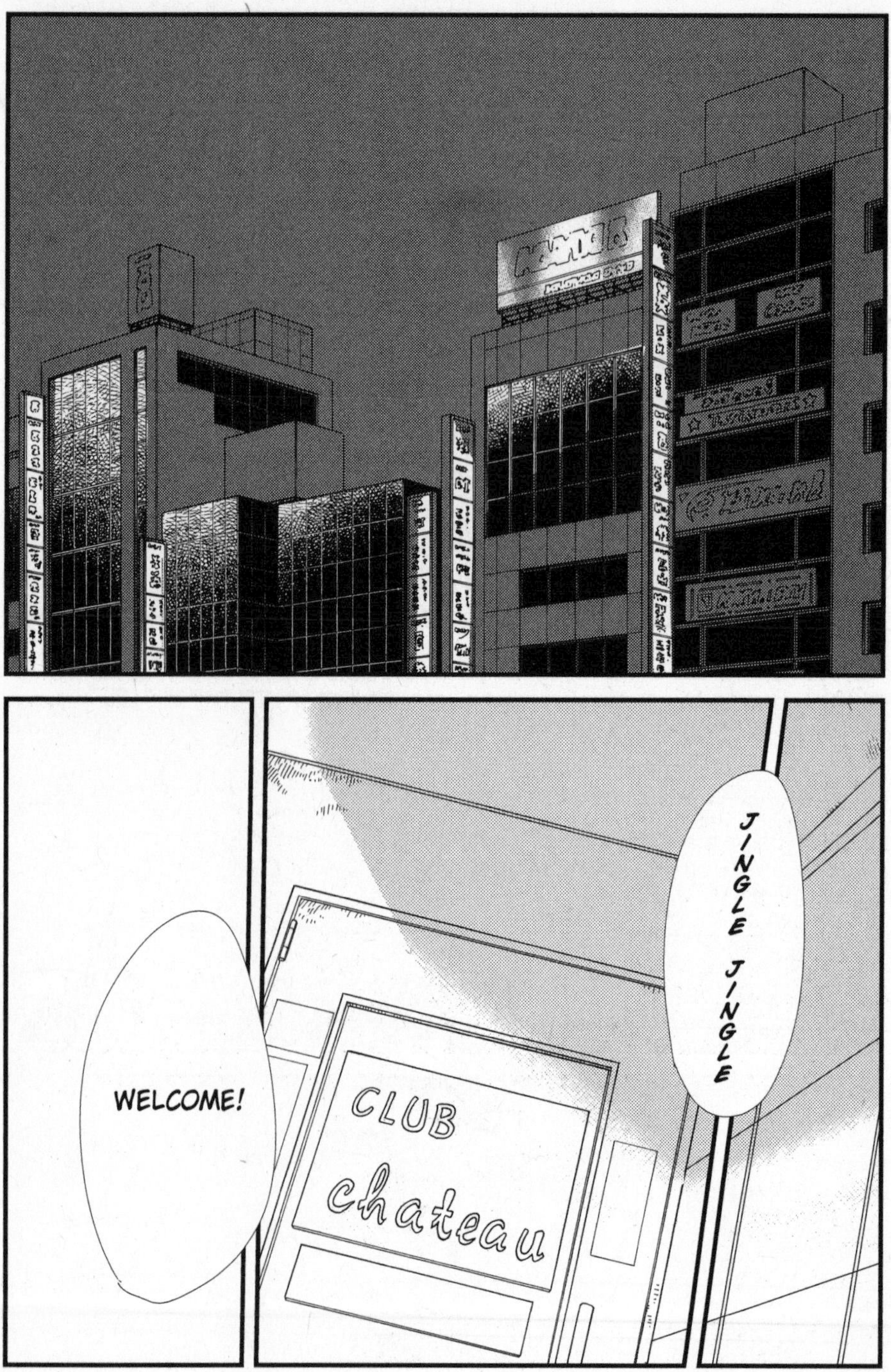
JINGLE JINGLE
CLUB chateau
WELCOME!

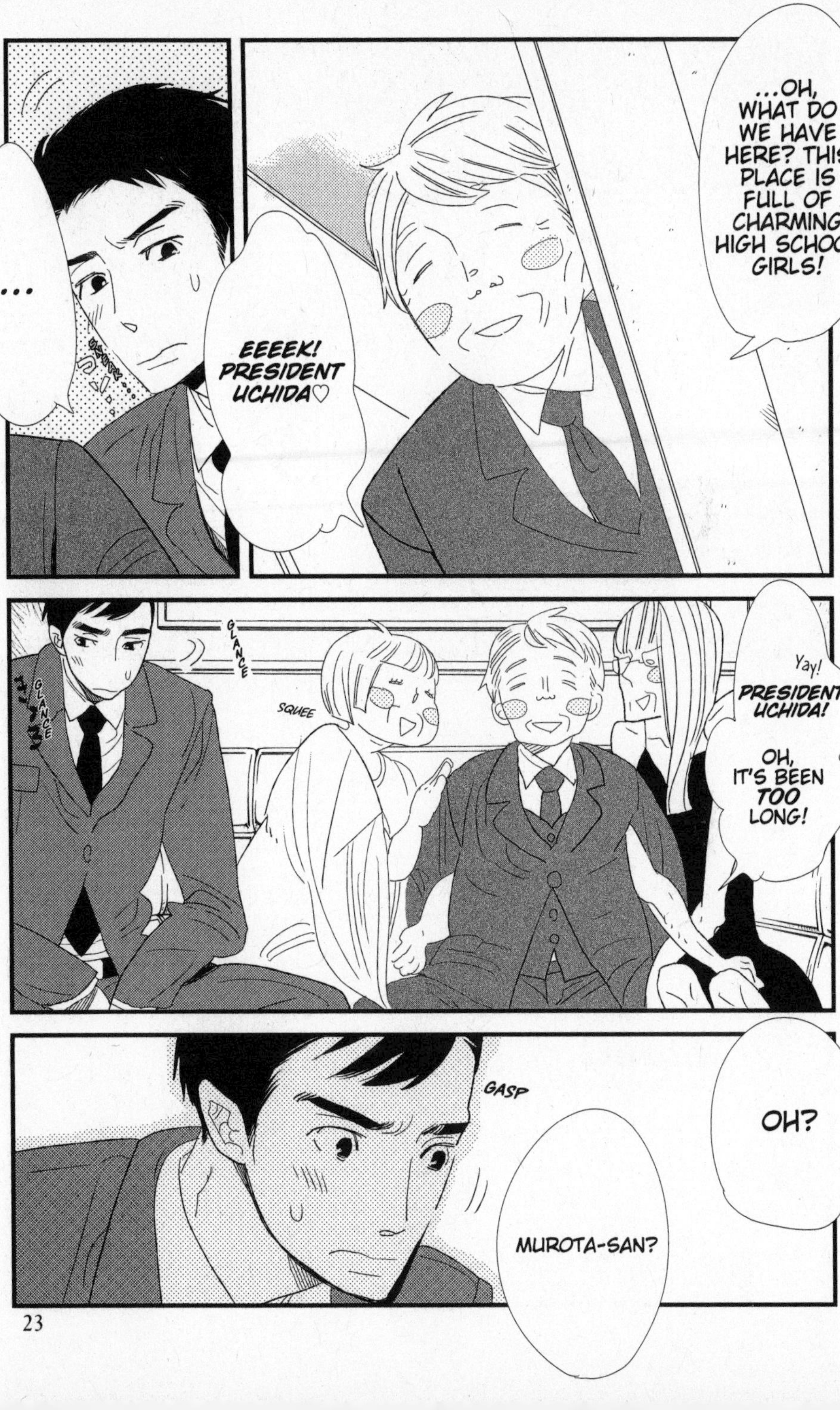
...OH, WHAT DO WE HAVE HERE? THIS PLACE IS FULL OF CHARMING HIGH SCHOOL GIRLS!
EEEEK! PRESIDENT UCHIDA♡
...
Yay! PRESIDENT UCHIDA!
OH, IT'S BEEN TOO LONG!
GLANCE
SQUEE
GLANCE
OH?
GASP
MUROTA-SAN?

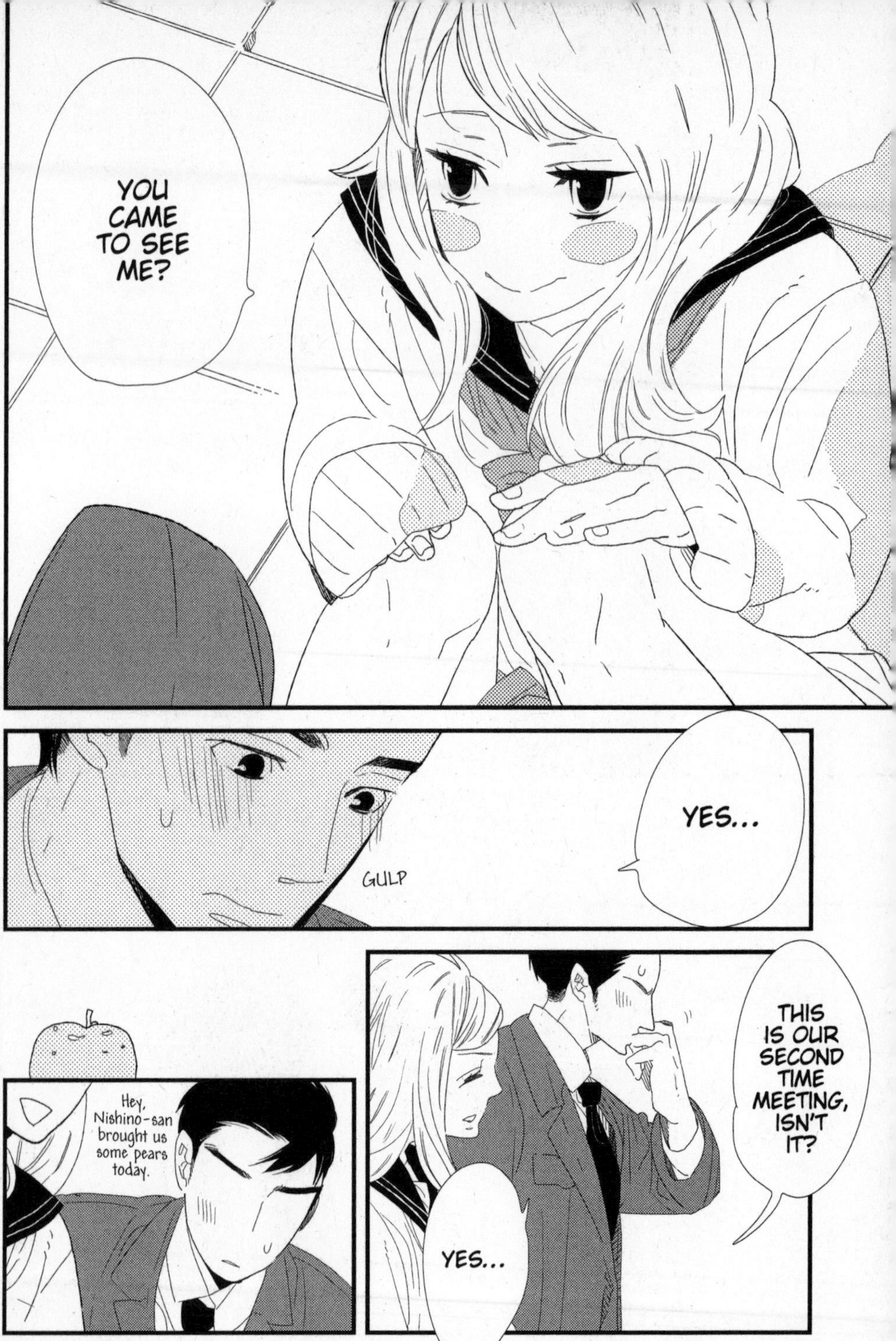
YOU CAME TO SEE ME?
YES...
GULP
THIS IS OUR SECOND TIME MEETING, ISN'T IT?
YES...
Hey, Nishino-san brought us some pears today.

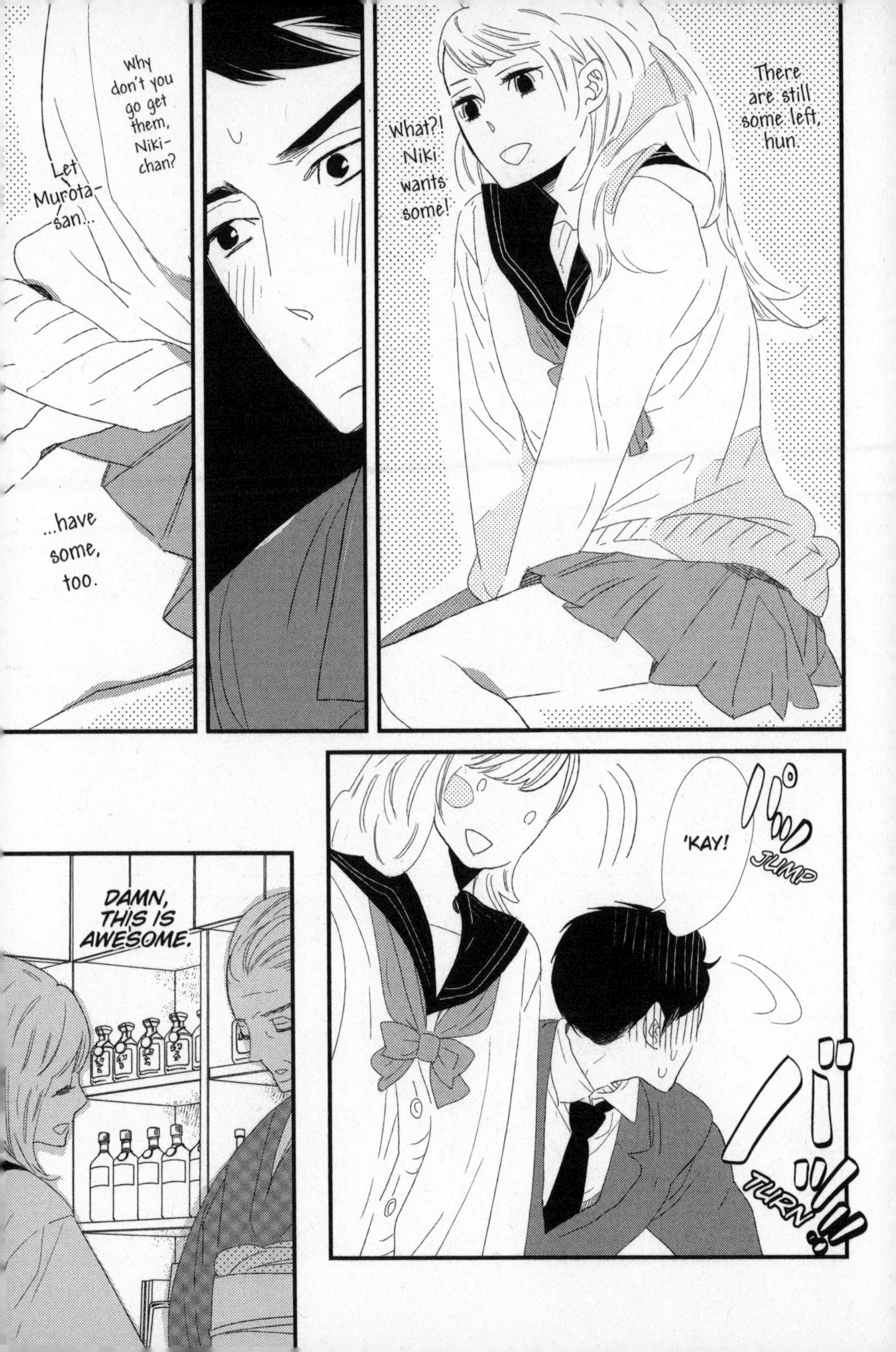
There are still some left, hun.
What?! Niki wants some!
Why don't you go get them, Niki-chan?
Let Murota-san...
...have some, too.
JUMP
'KAY!
TURN
DAMN, THIS IS AWESOME.

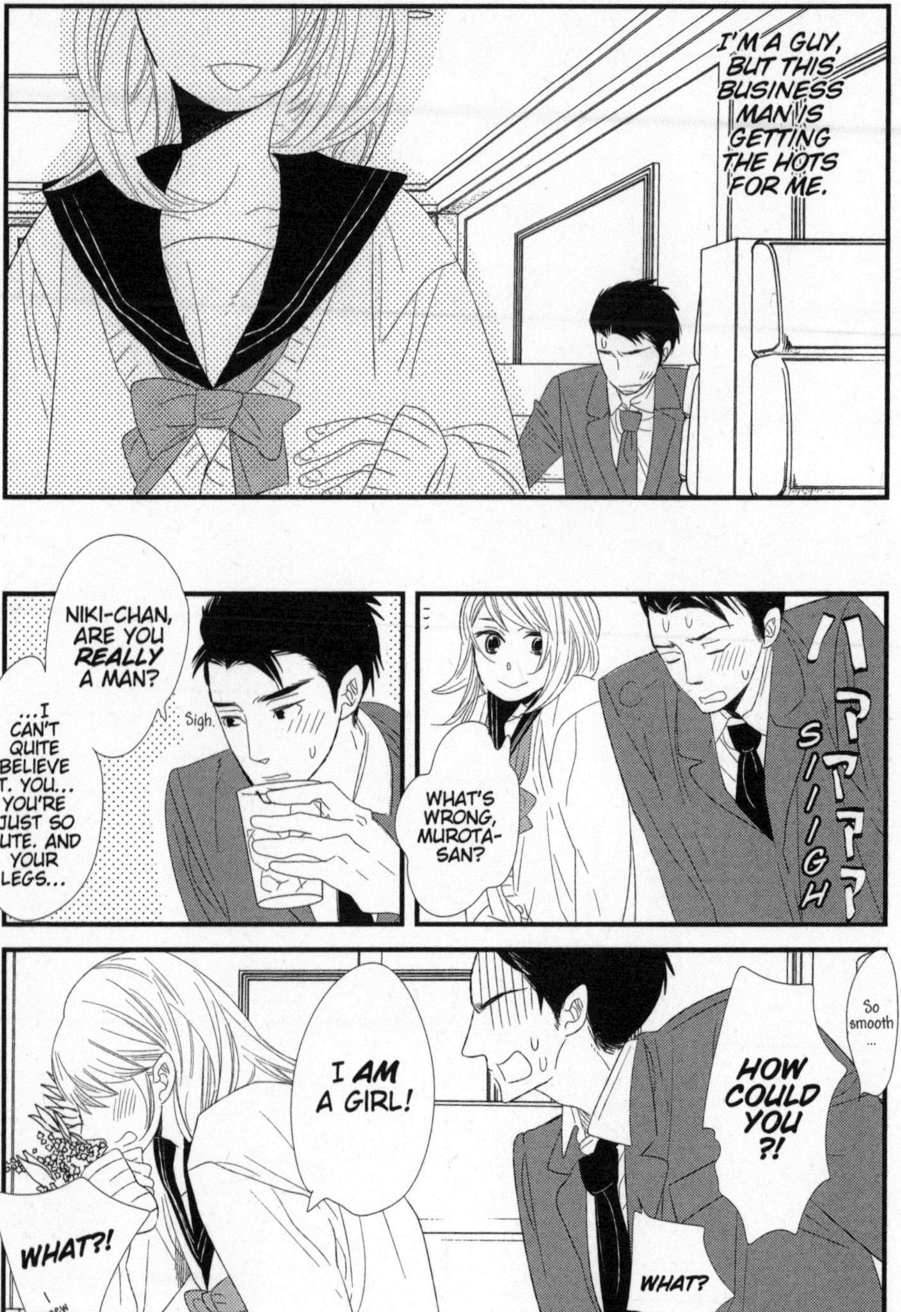
I'M A GUY, BUT THIS BUSINESS MAN IS GETTING THE HOTS FOR ME.
ハアアア
SIIIGH
WHAT'S WRONG, MUROTA-SAN?
NIKI-CHAN, ARE YOU *REALLY* A MAN?
Sigh.
...I CAN'T QUITE BELIEVE IT. YOU... YOU'RE JUST SO CUTE. AND YOUR LEGS...
So smooth ...
HOW COULD YOU ?!
WHAT?
I *AM* A GIRL!
WHAT?!
I knew it!

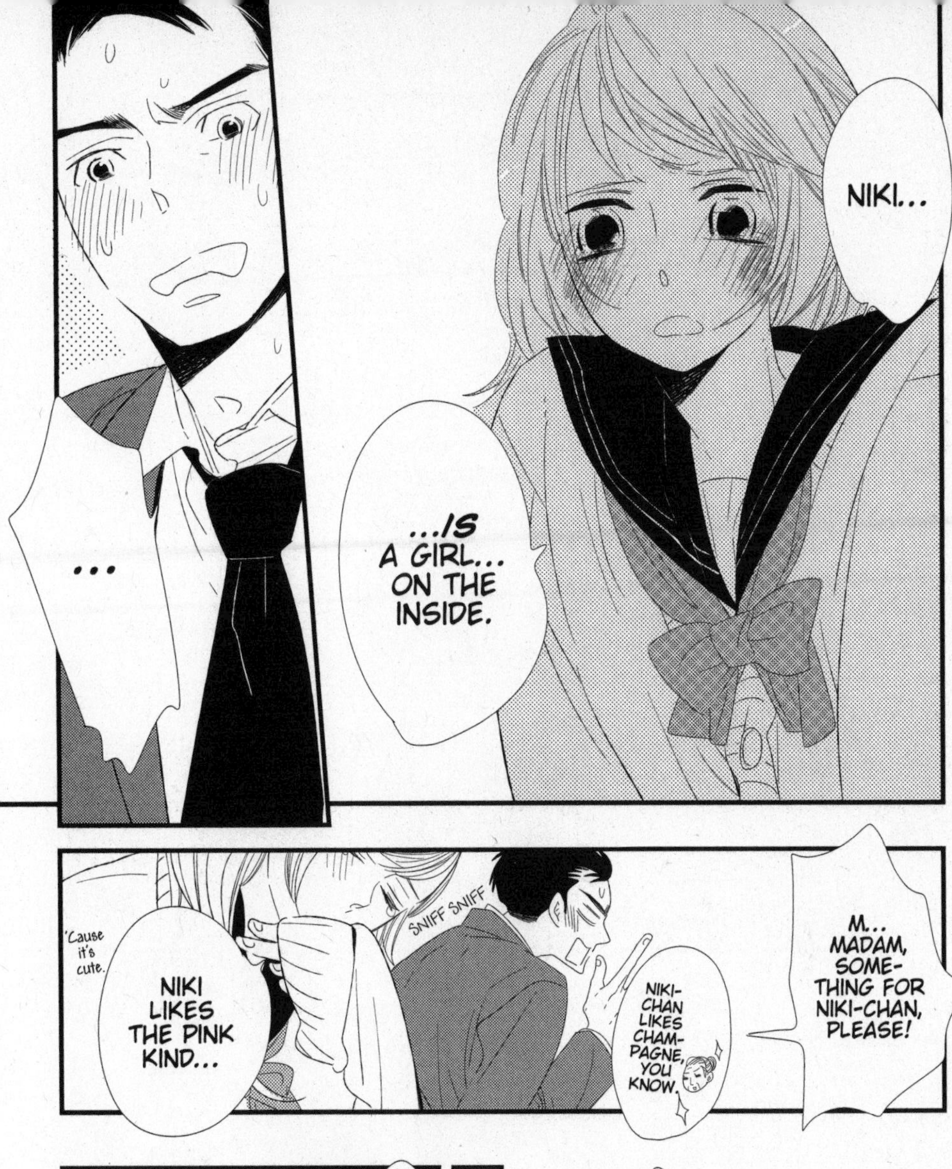

NIKI...
...IS A GIRL... ON THE INSIDE.
...
M... MADAM, SOMETHING FOR NIKI-CHAN, PLEASE!
NIKI-CHAN LIKES CHAMPAGNE, YOU KNOW.
SNIFF SNIFF
NIKI LIKES THE PINK KIND...
'Cause it's cute.
MUROTA, PINK DOM IS 120,000 YEN.*
We're paying separately today.
I DON'T MIND... 120 ?!
For one bottle ?!
TUG...

*Dom Perignon Rosé, about $1,200 USD.

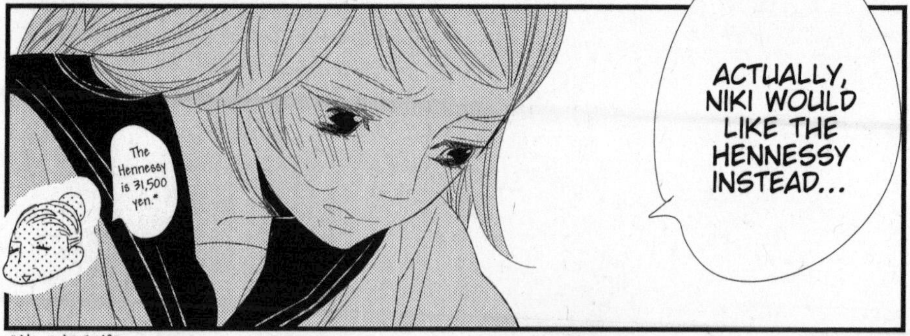
ACTUALLY, NIKI WOULD LIKE THE HENNESSY INSTEAD...
The Hennessy is 31,500 yen.*

*About $315 USD.

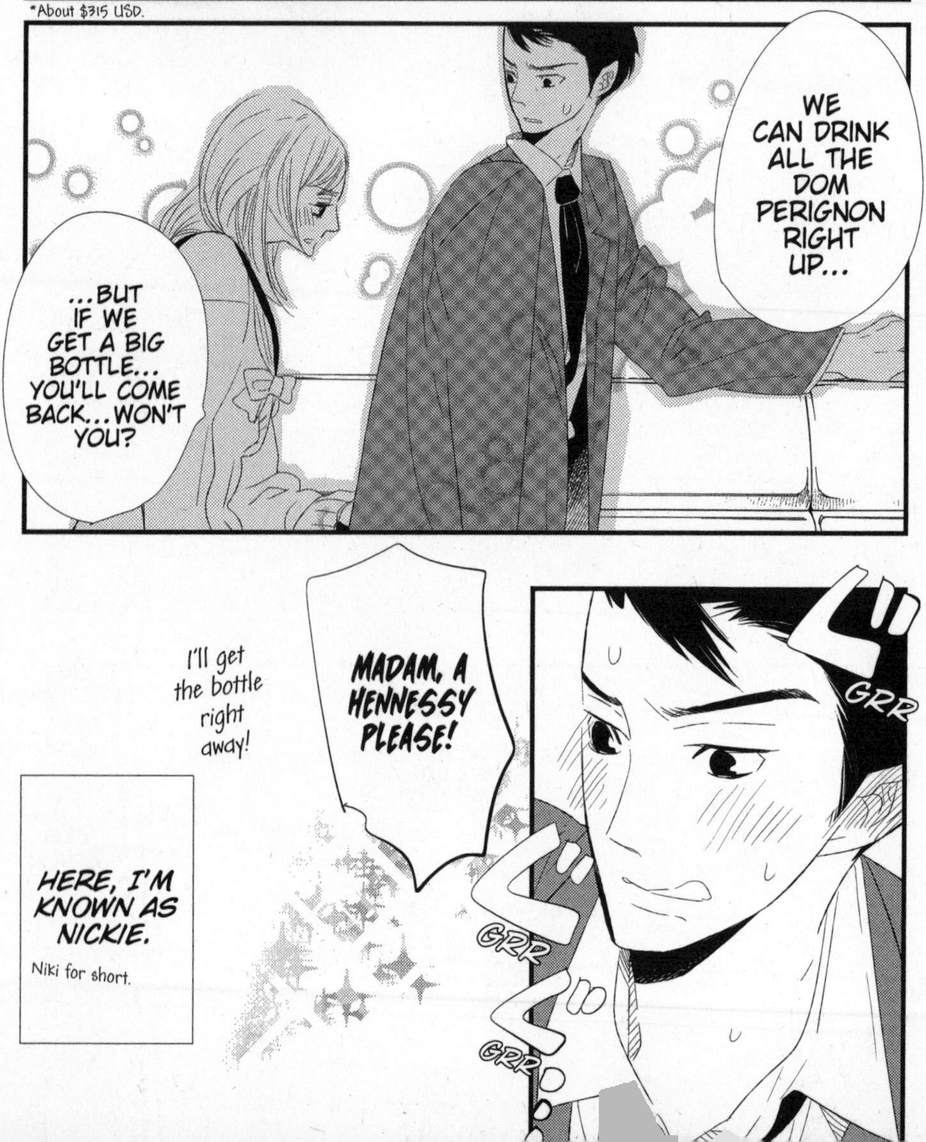
WE CAN DRINK ALL THE DOM PERIGNON RIGHT UP...
...BUT IF WE GET A BIG BOTTLE... YOU'LL COME BACK...WON'T YOU?
GRR
MADAM, A HENNESSY PLEASE!
I'll get the bottle right away!
GRR
GRR
HERE, I'M KNOWN AS NICKIE.
Niki for short.

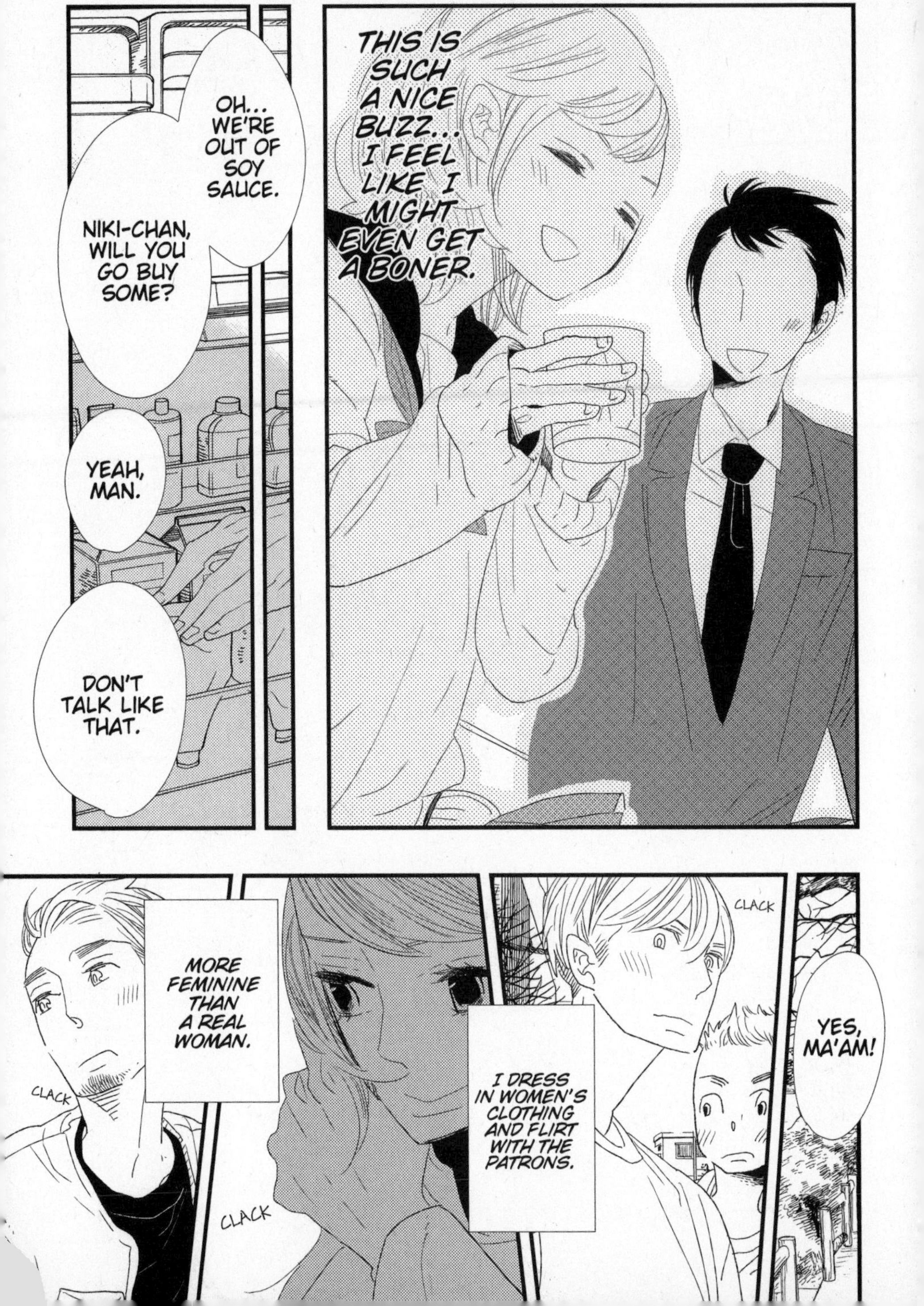
THIS IS SUCH A NICE BUZZ... I FEEL LIKE I MIGHT EVEN GET A BONER.
OH... WE'RE OUT OF SOY SAUCE.
NIKI-CHAN, WILL YOU GO BUY SOME?
YEAH, MAN.
DON'T TALK LIKE THAT.
YES, MA'AM!
CLACK
I DRESS IN WOMEN'S CLOTHING AND FLIRT WITH THE PATRONS.
MORE FEMININE THAN A REAL WOMAN.
CLACK
CLACK

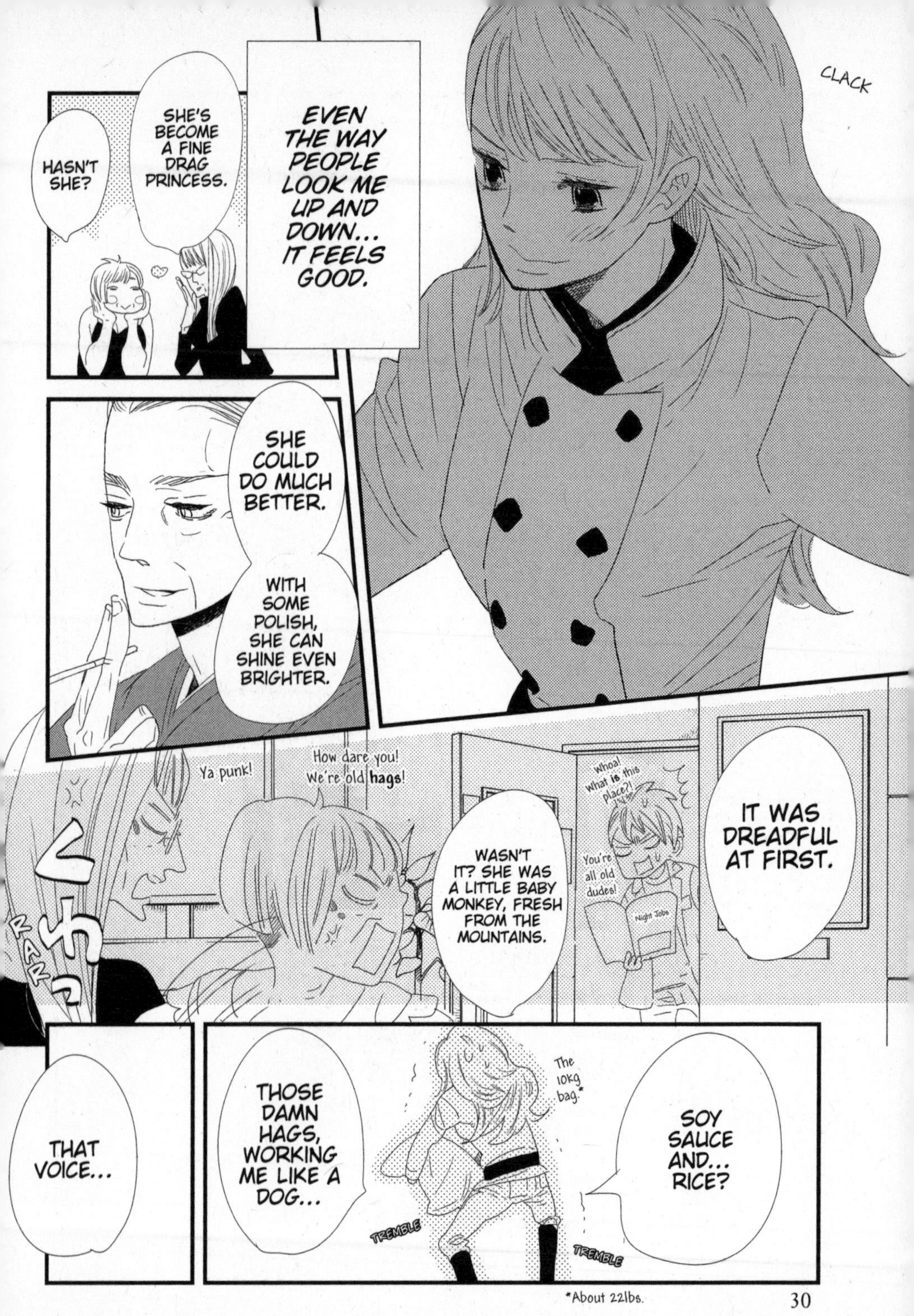
CLACK
EVEN THE WAY PEOPLE LOOK ME UP AND DOWN... IT FEELS GOOD.
SHE'S BECOME A FINE DRAG PRINCESS.
HASN'T SHE?
SHE COULD DO MUCH BETTER.
WITH SOME POLISH, SHE CAN SHINE EVEN BRIGHTER.
IT WAS DREADFUL AT FIRST.
Whoa! What is this place?!
You're all old dudes!
Night Jobs
WASN'T IT? SHE WAS A LITTLE BABY MONKEY, FRESH FROM THE MOUNTAINS.
How dare you! We're old **hags**!
Ya punk!
くわっ
RAR
SOY SAUCE AND... RICE?
The 10kg bag.*
TREMBLE
TREMBLE
THOSE DAMN HAGS, WORKING ME LIKE A DOG...
THAT VOICE...

*About 22lbs.

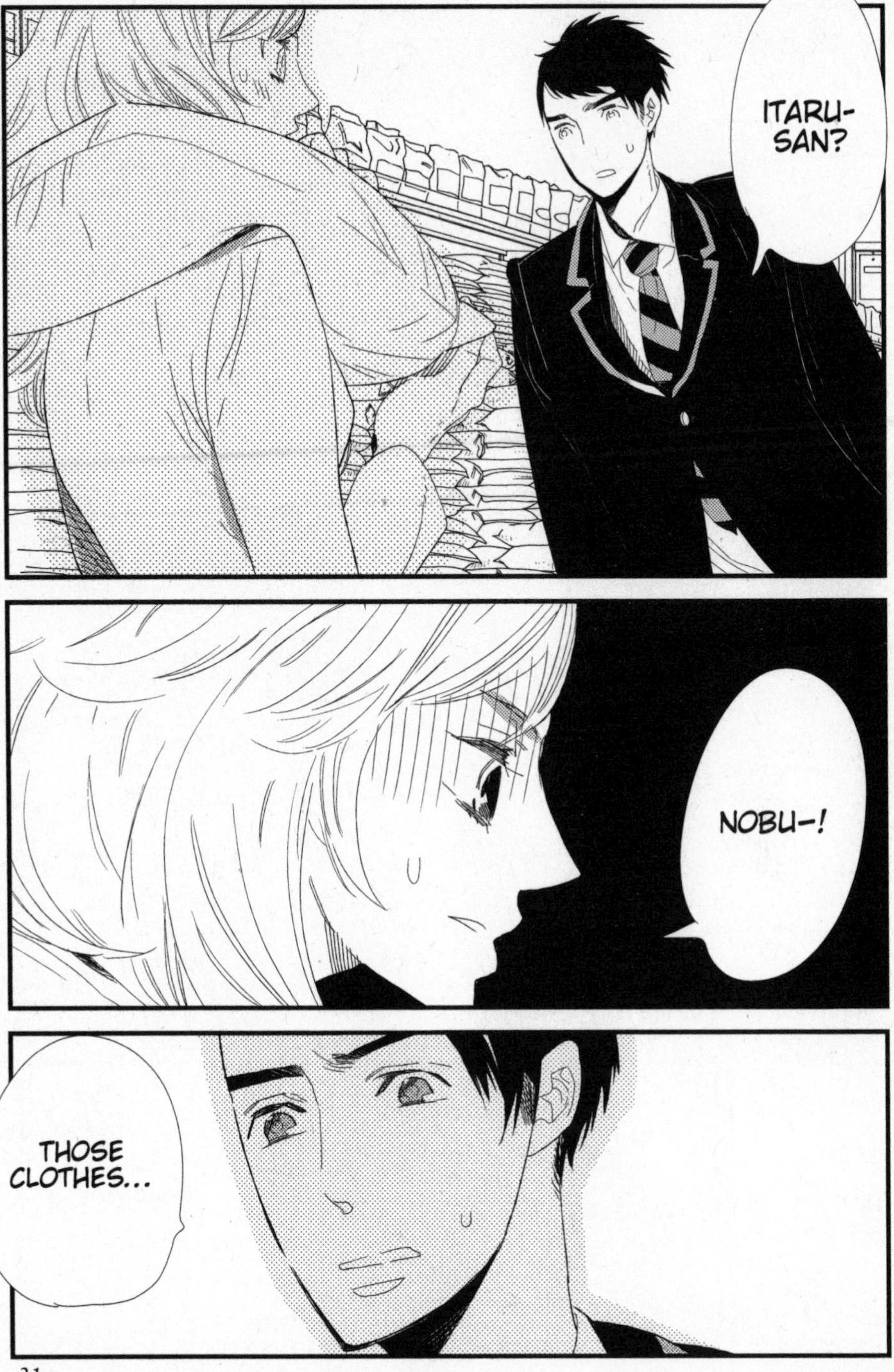
ITARU-SAN?
NOBU-!
THOSE CLOTHES...

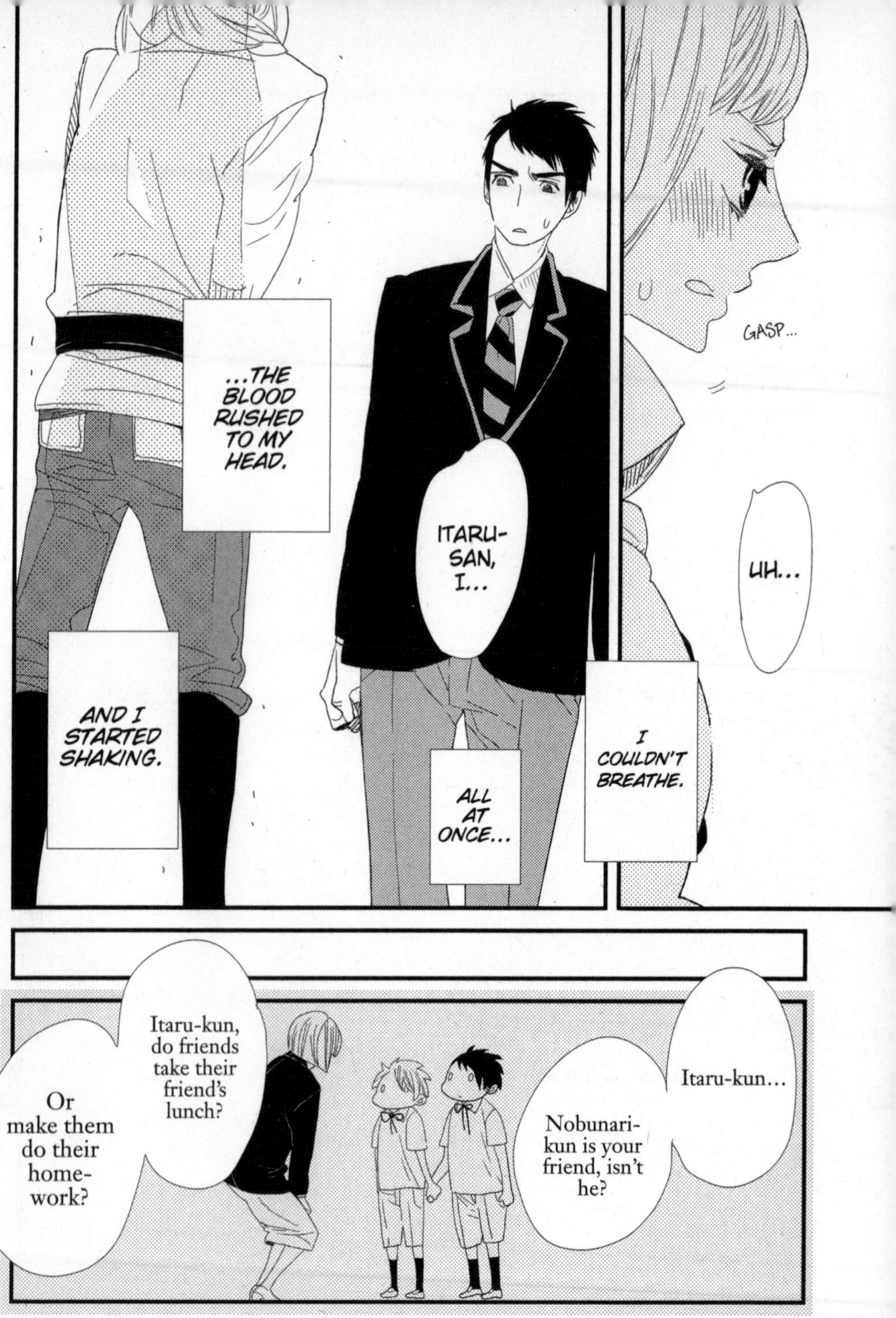
GASP...
UH...
ITARU-SAN, I...
I COULDN'T BREATHE.
ALL AT ONCE...
...THE BLOOD RUSHED TO MY HEAD.
AND I STARTED SHAKING.
Itaru-kun...
Nobunari-kun is your friend, isn't he?
Itaru-kun, do friends take their friend's lunch?
Or make them do their home-work?

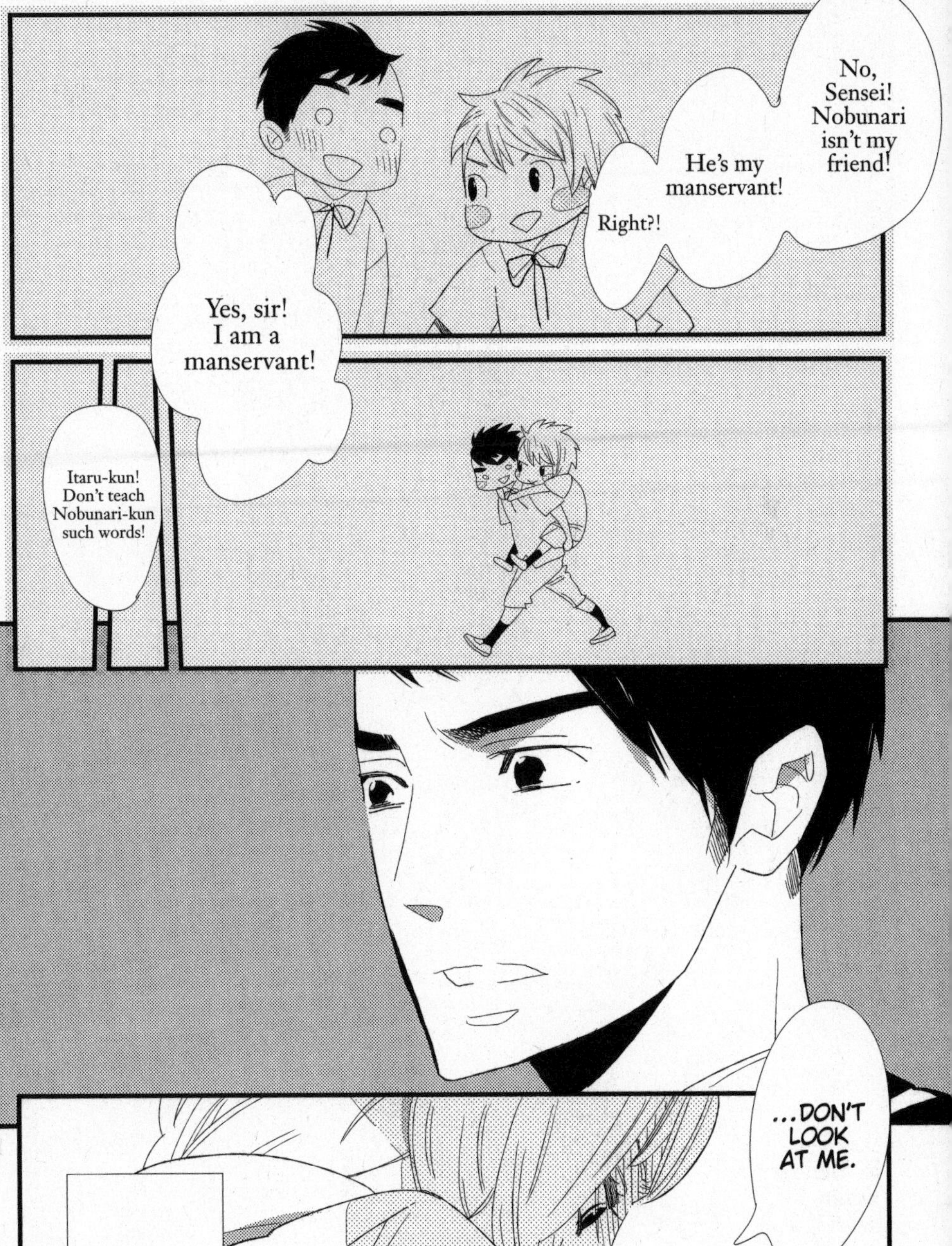
No, Sensei! Nobunari isn't my friend!
He's my manservant!
Right?!
Yes, sir! I am a manservant!
Itaru-kun! Don't teach Nobunari-kun such words!
...DON'T LOOK AT ME.
MY LEGS...

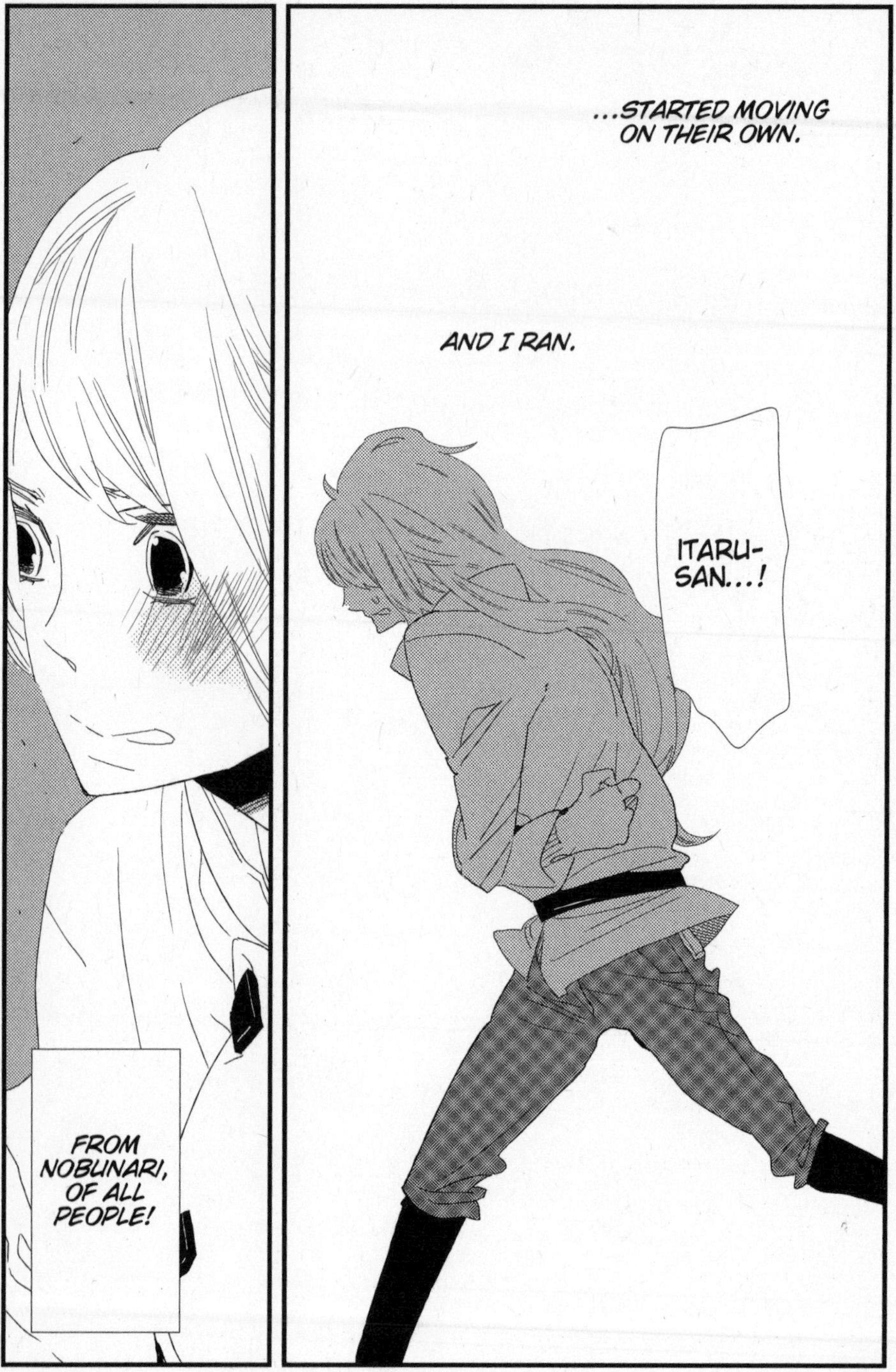
...STARTED MOVING ON THEIR OWN.
AND I RAN.
ITARU-SAN...!
FROM NOBUNARI, OF ALL PEOPLE!

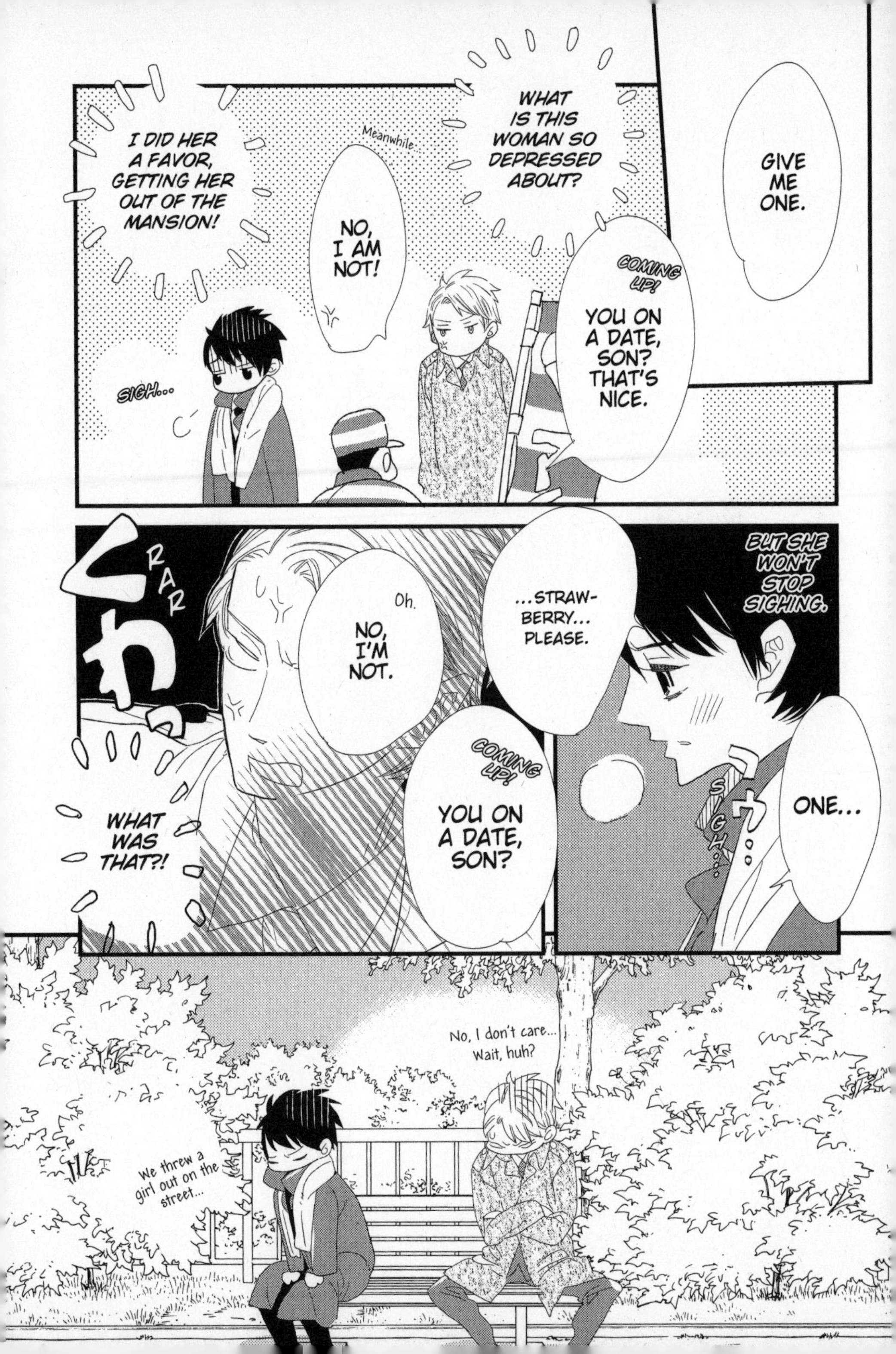
GIVE ME ONE.
WHAT IS THIS WOMAN SO DEPRESSED ABOUT?
COMING UP!
YOU ON A DATE, SON? THAT'S NICE.
Meanwhile...
NO, I AM NOT!
I DID HER A FAVOR, GETTING HER OUT OF THE MANSION!
SIGH...
BUT SHE WON'T STOP SIGHING.
SIGH...
ONE...
...STRAWBERRY... PLEASE.
COMING UP!
YOU ON A DATE, SON?
Oh.
NO, I'M NOT.
RAR
WHAT WAS THAT?!
No, I don't care... Wait, huh?
We threw a girl out on the street...

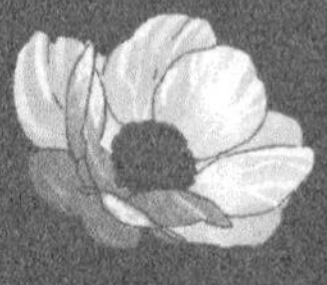

The prince in his dark days

Hico Yamanaka

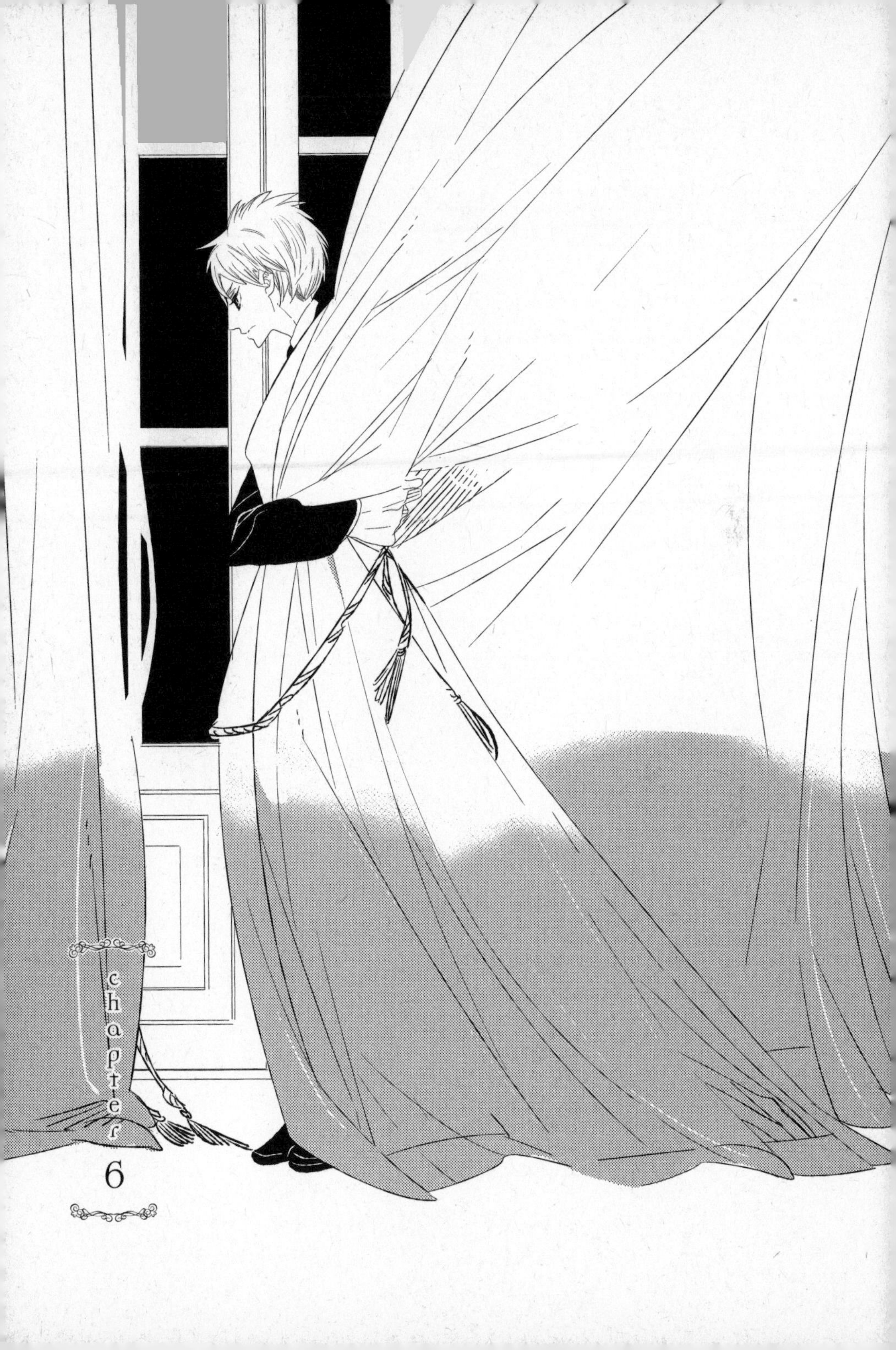
chapter
6

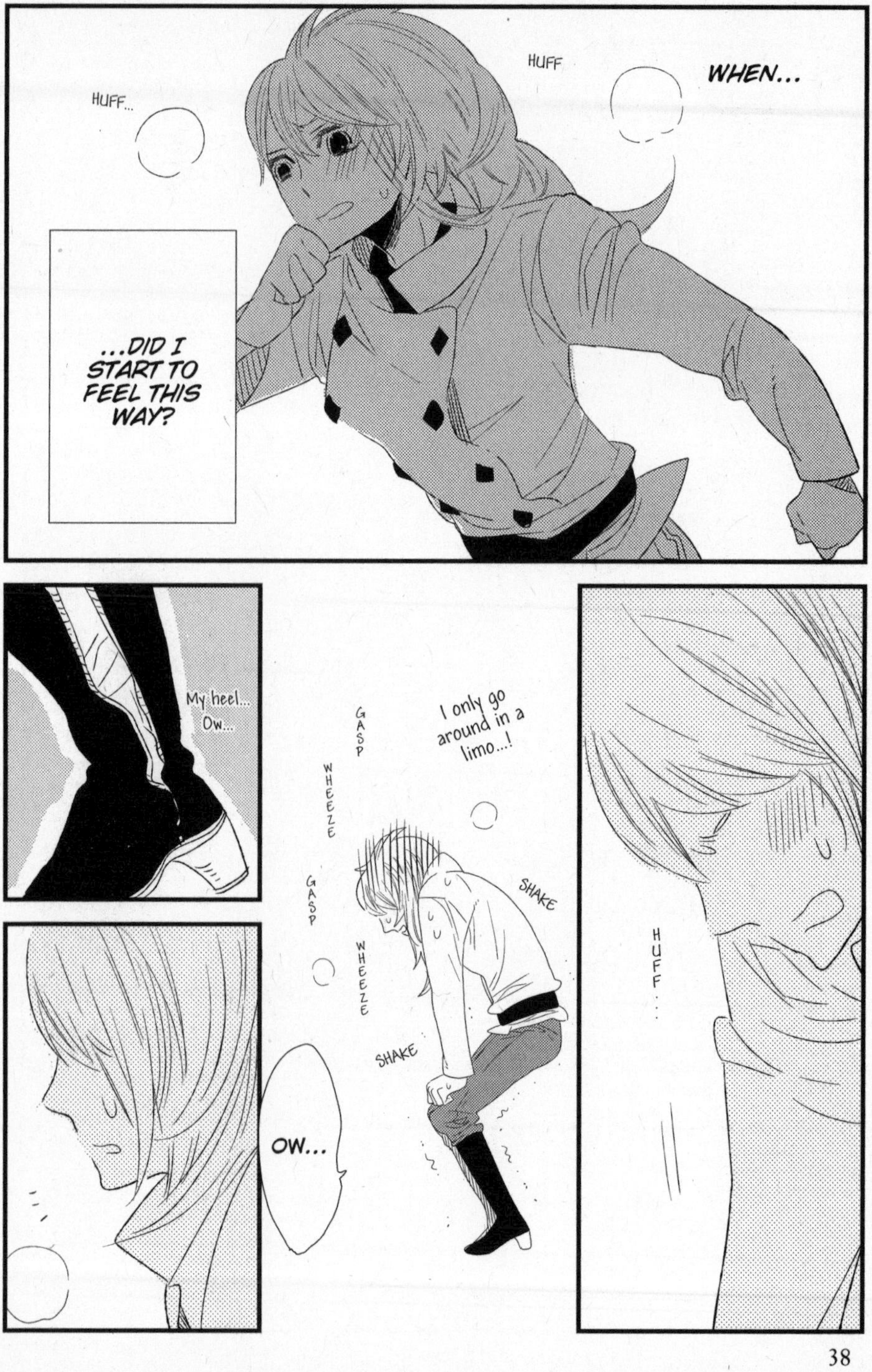
WHEN...
HUFF
HUFF...
...DID I START TO FEEL THIS WAY?
HUFF...
I only go around in a limo...!
SHAKE
GASP
WHEEZE
GASP
WHEEZE
SHAKE
OW...
My heel... Ow...

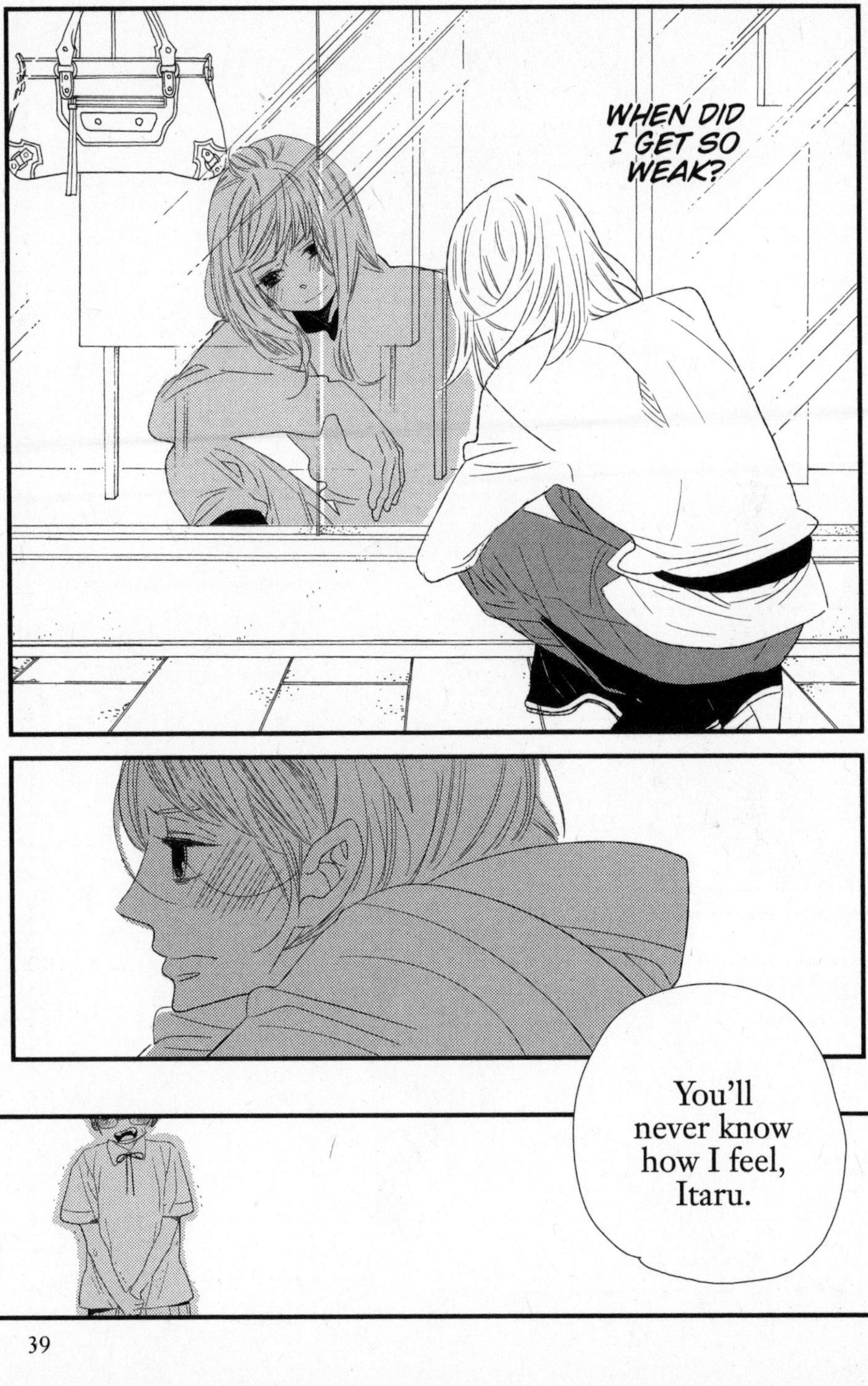
WHEN DID I GET SO WEAK?
You'll never know how I feel, Itaru.

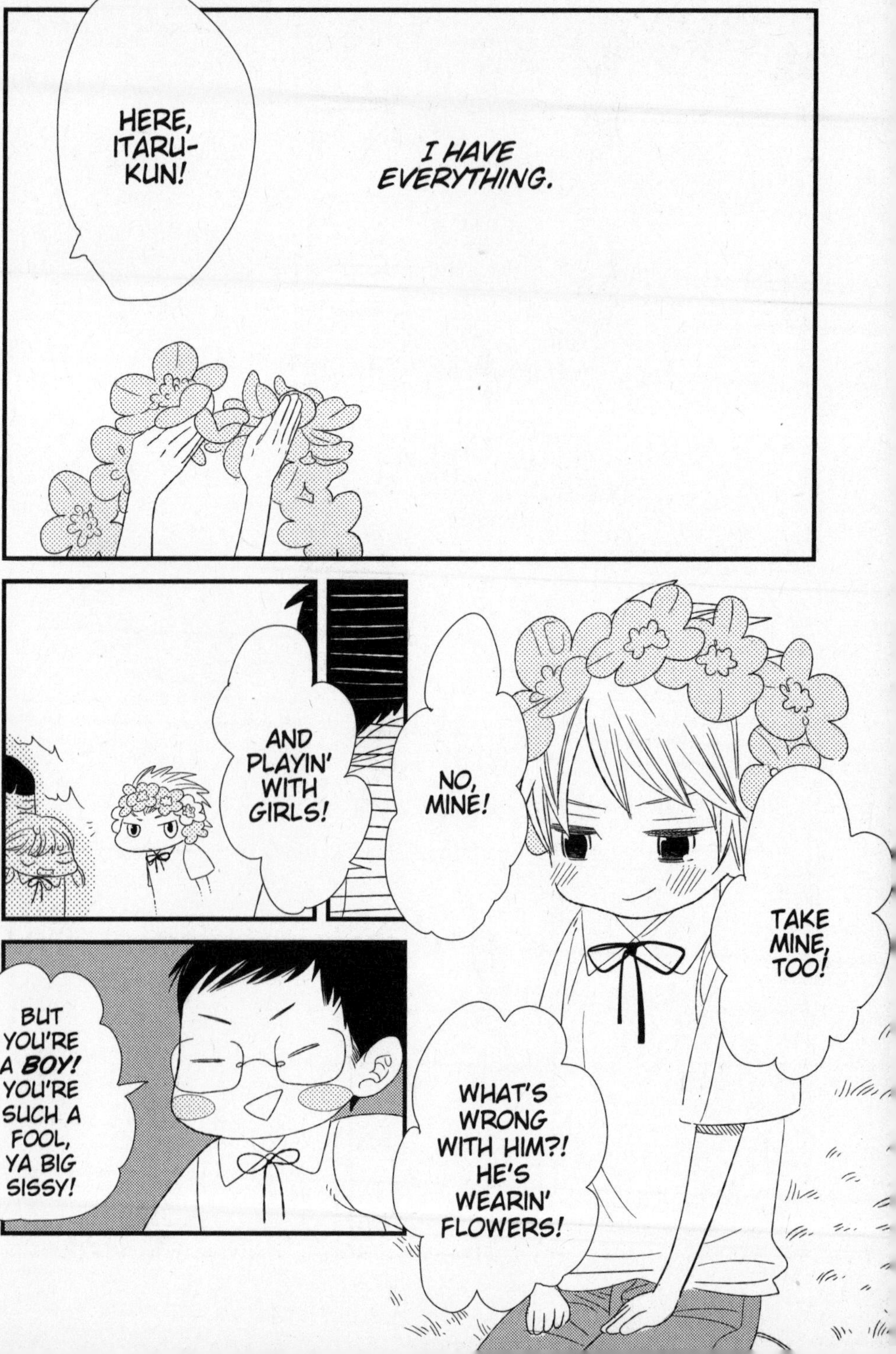
HERE, ITARU-KUN!
I HAVE EVERYTHING.
TAKE MINE, TOO!
NO, MINE!
WHAT'S WRONG WITH HIM?! HE'S WEARIN' FLOWERS!
AND PLAYIN' WITH GIRLS!
BUT YOU'RE A BOY! YOU'RE SUCH A FOOL, YA BIG SISSY!

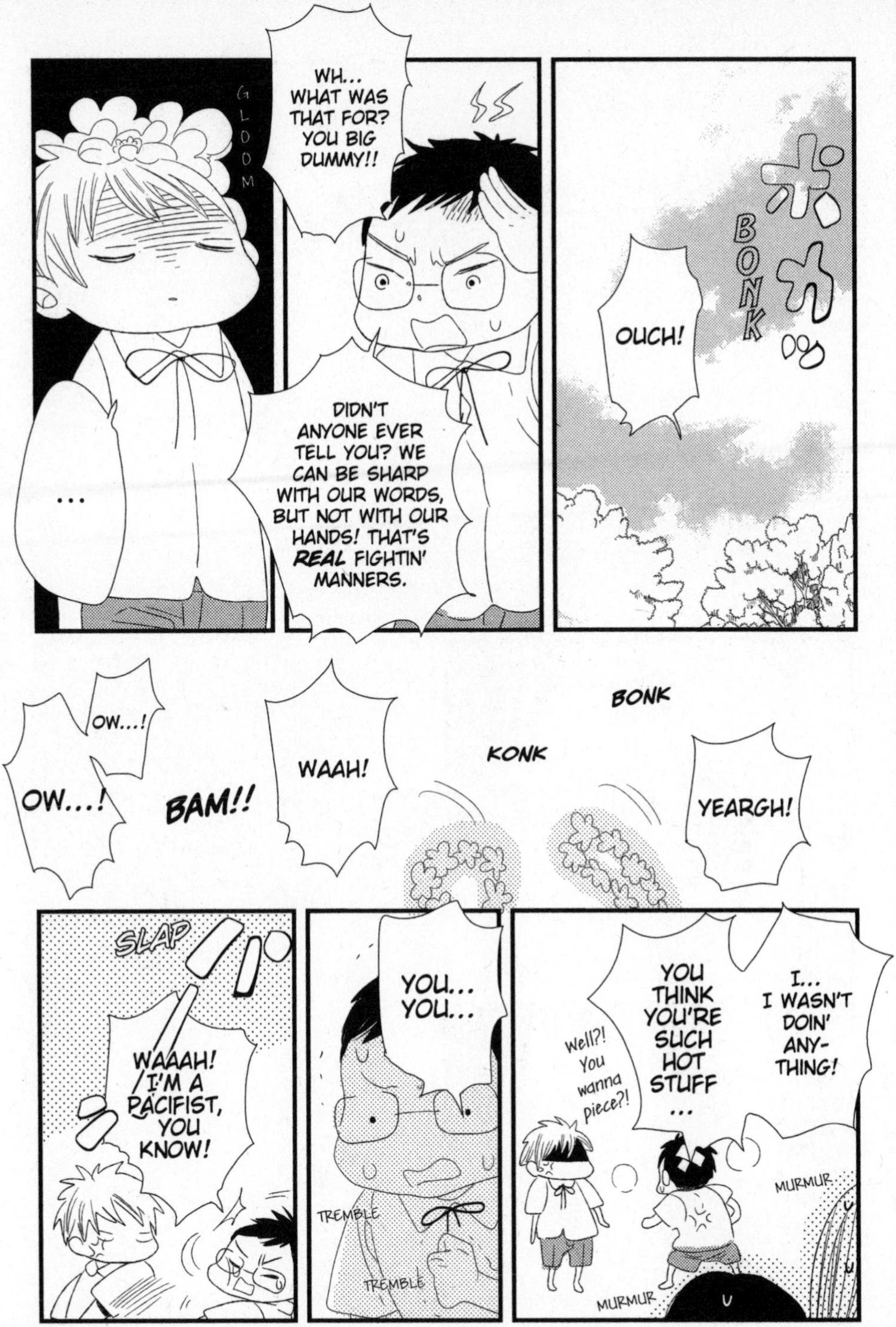
BONK
OUCH!
WH... WHAT WAS THAT FOR? YOU BIG DUMMY!!
DIDN'T ANYONE EVER TELL YOU? WE CAN BE SHARP WITH OUR WORDS, BUT NOT WITH OUR HANDS! THAT'S ***REAL*** FIGHTIN' MANNERS.
GLOOM
...
YEARGH!
BONK
KONK
WAAH!
BAM!!
OW...!
OW...!
I... I WASN'T DOIN' ANY-THING!
YOU THINK YOU'RE SUCH HOT STUFF...
Well?! You wanna piece?!
MURMUR
MURMUR
YOU... YOU...
TREMBLE
TREMBLE
SLAP
WAAAH! I'M A PACIFIST, YOU KNOW!

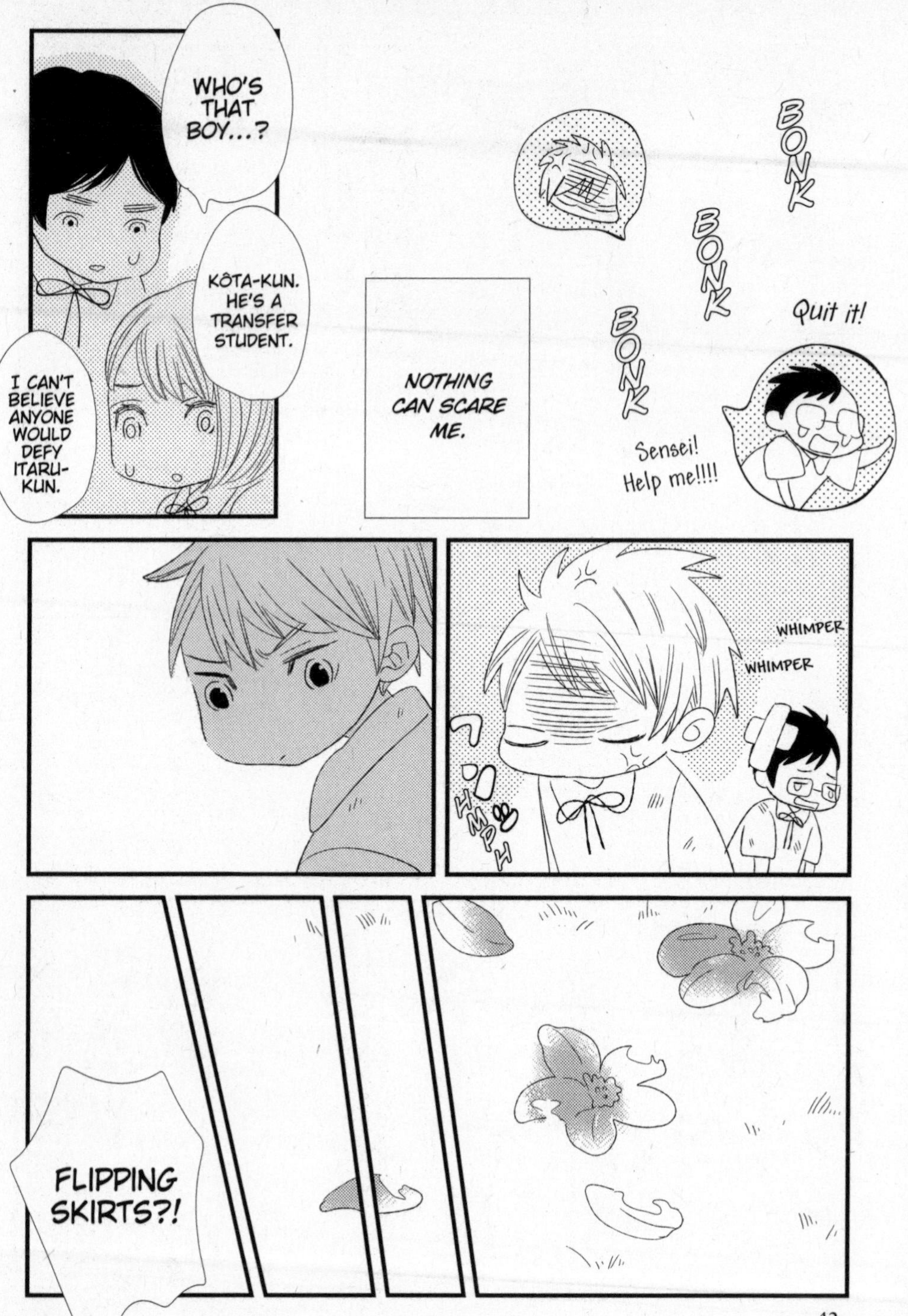
BONK
BONK
BONK
Quit it!
Sensei! Help me!!!!
NOTHING CAN SCARE ME.
WHO'S THAT BOY...?
KÔTA-KUN. HE'S A TRANSFER STUDENT.
I CAN'T BELIEVE ANYONE WOULD DEFY ITARU-KUN.
WHIMPER
WHIMPER
HMPH
FLIPPING SKIRTS?!

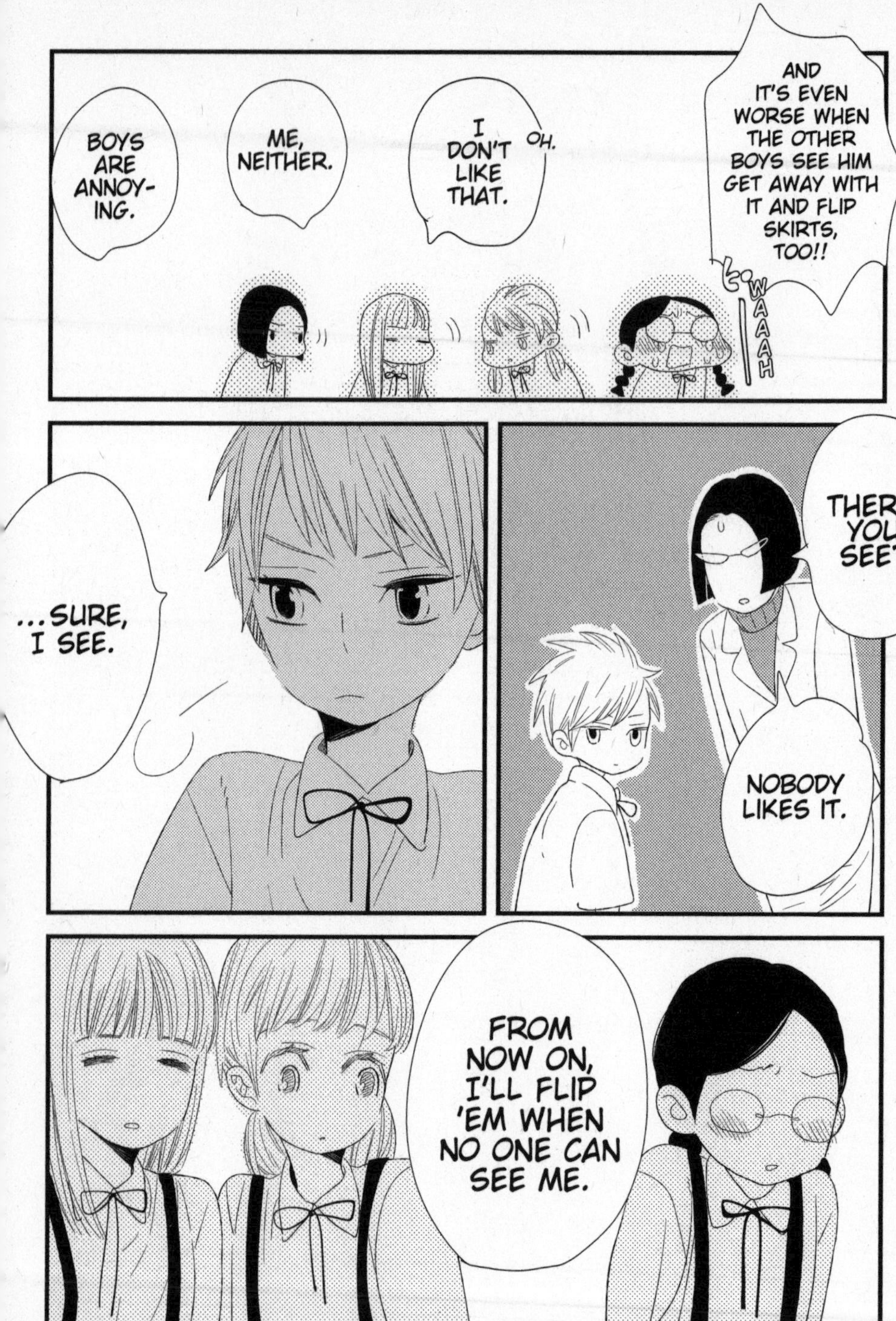
AND IT'S EVEN WORSE WHEN THE OTHER BOYS SEE HIM GET AWAY WITH IT AND FLIP SKIRTS, TOO!!
WAAAAH
OH.
I DON'T LIKE THAT.
ME, NEITHER.
BOYS ARE ANNOY-ING.
THERE, YOU SEE?
NOBODY LIKES IT.
...SURE, I SEE.
FROM NOW ON, I'LL FLIP 'EM WHEN NO ONE CAN SEE ME.

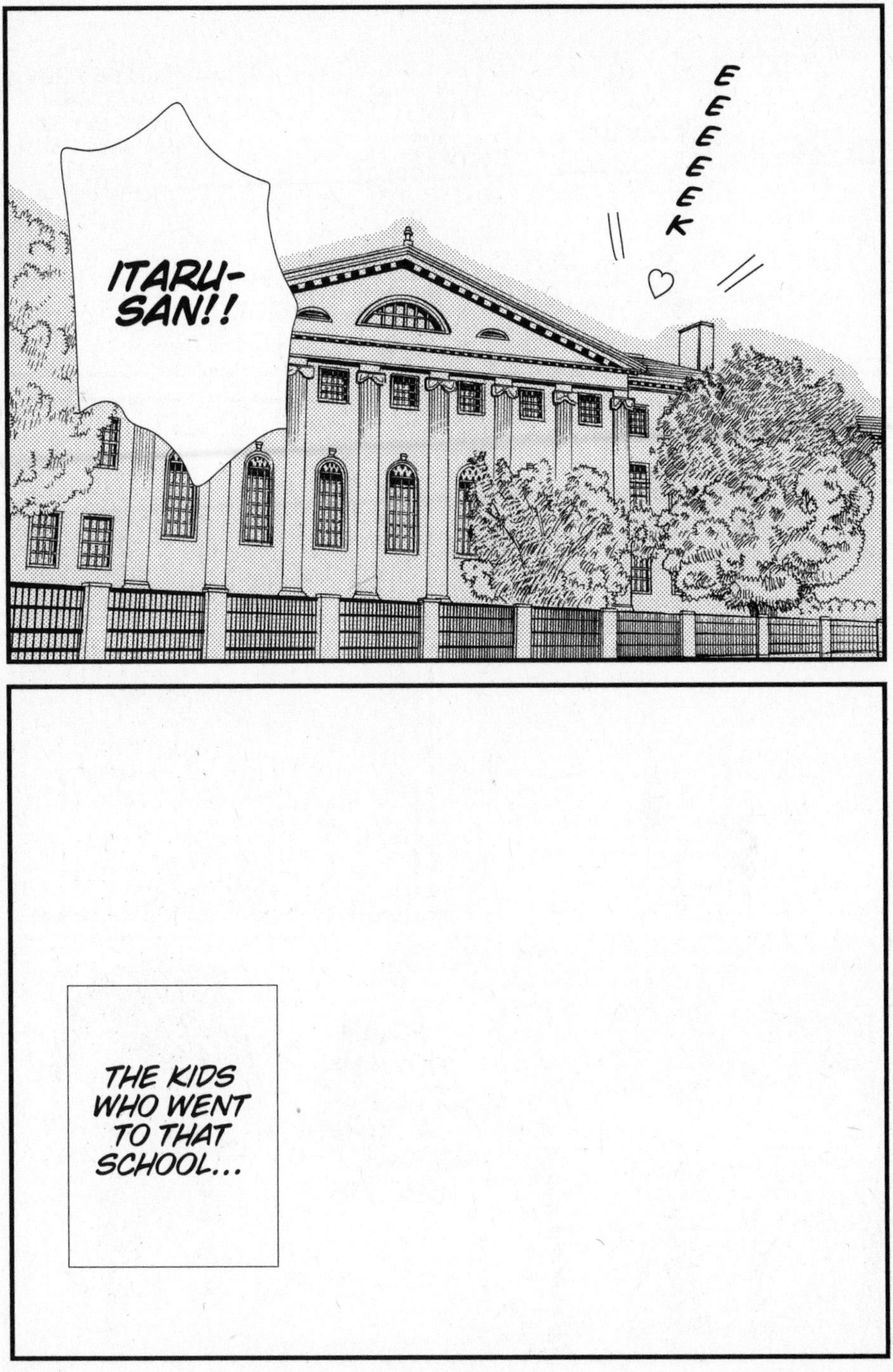
EEEEEK
ITARU-SAN!!
THE KIDS WHO WENT TO THAT SCHOOL...

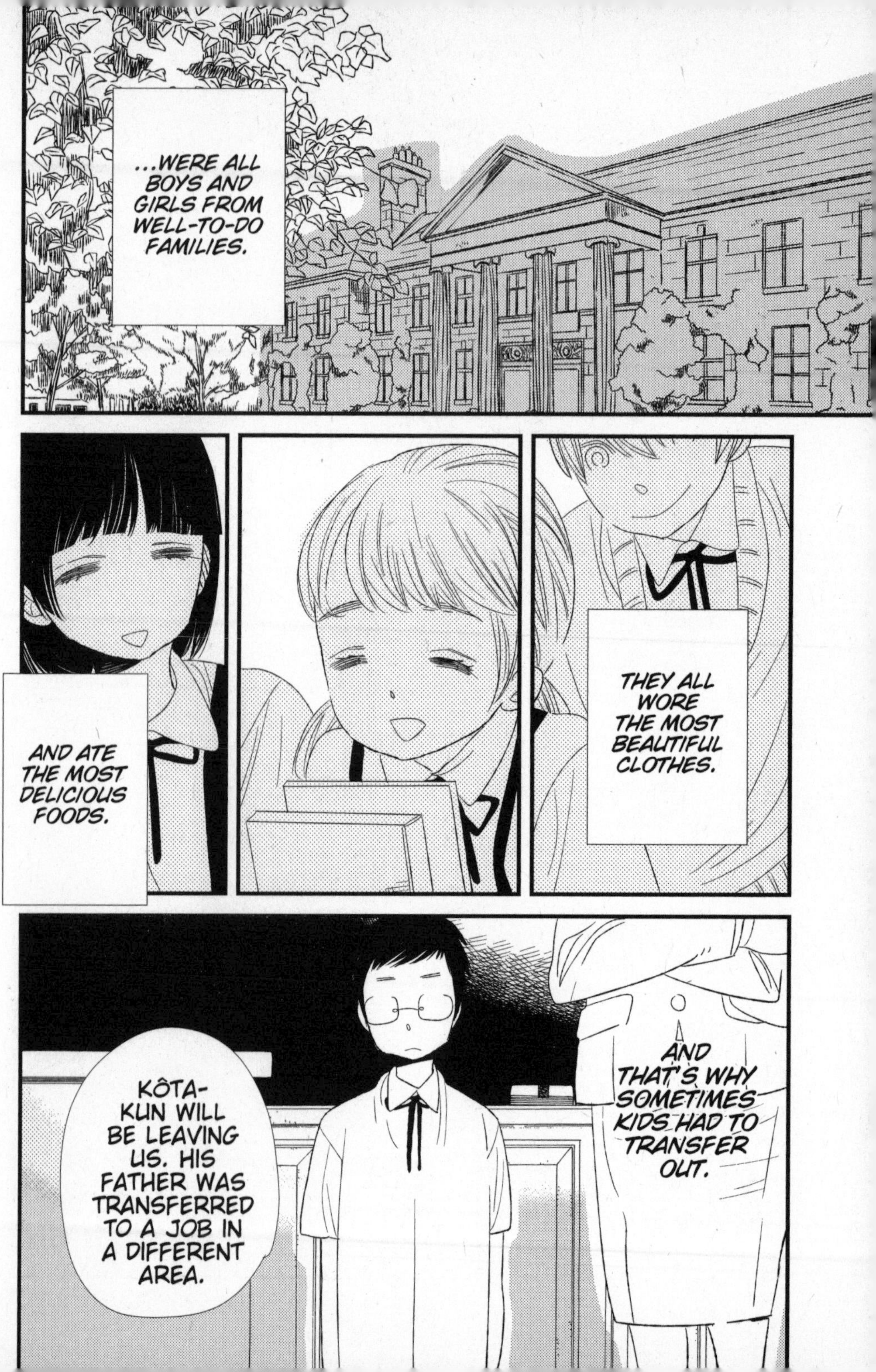
...WERE ALL BOYS AND GIRLS FROM WELL-TO-DO FAMILIES.
THEY ALL WORE THE MOST BEAUTIFUL CLOTHES.
AND ATE THE MOST DELICIOUS FOODS.
AND THAT'S WHY SOMETIMES KIDS HAD TO TRANSFER OUT.
KÔTA-KUN WILL BE LEAVING US. HIS FATHER WAS TRANSFERRED TO A JOB IN A DIFFERENT AREA.

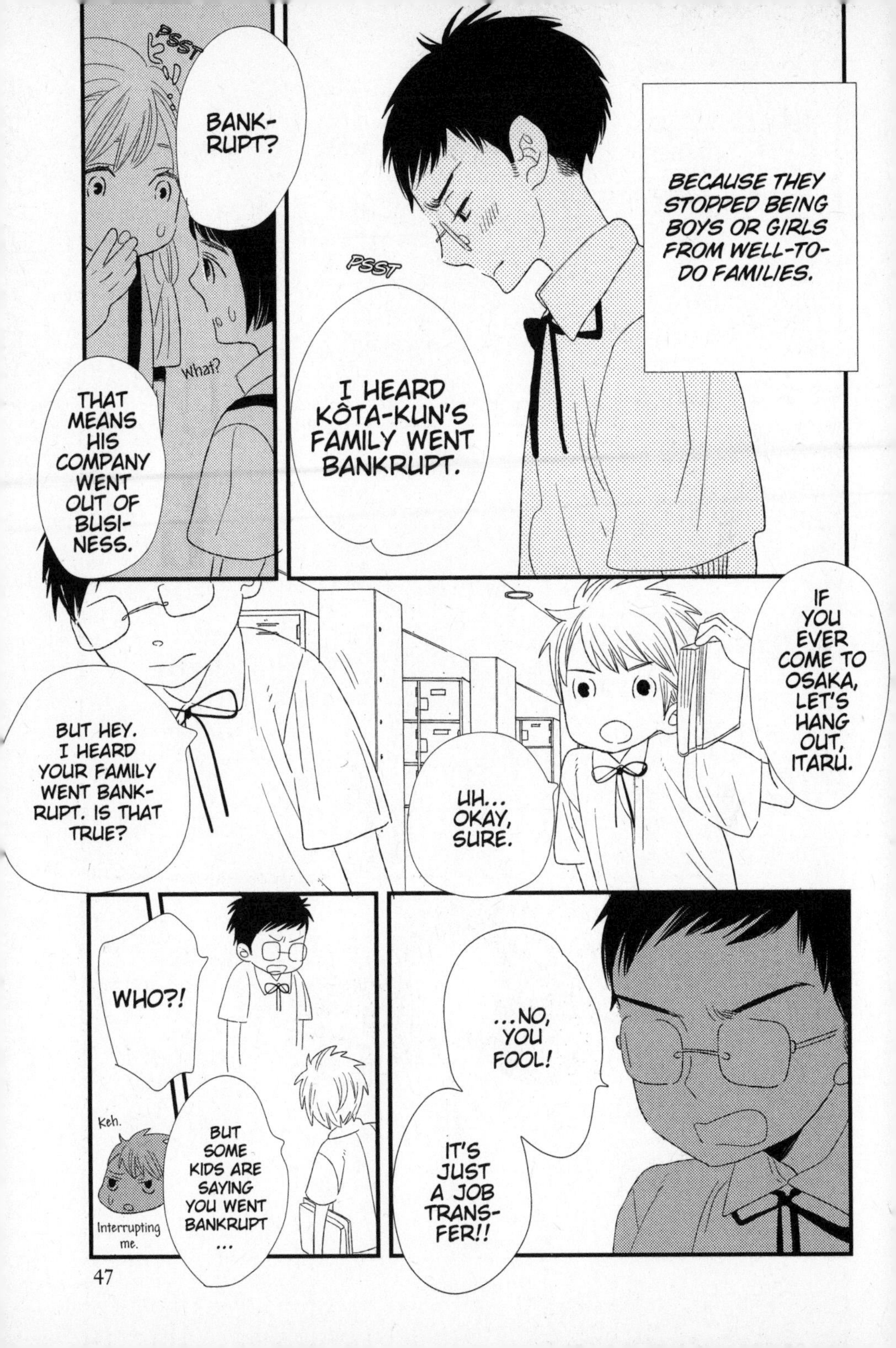
BECAUSE THEY STOPPED BEING BOYS OR GIRLS FROM WELL-TO-DO FAMILIES.
PSST
I HEARD KÔTA-KUN'S FAMILY WENT BANKRUPT.
PSST
BANK-RUPT?
What?
THAT MEANS HIS COMPANY WENT OUT OF BUSI-NESS.
IF YOU EVER COME TO OSAKA, LET'S HANG OUT, ITARU.
UH... OKAY, SURE.
BUT HEY. I HEARD YOUR FAMILY WENT BANK-RUPT. IS THAT TRUE?
...NO, YOU FOOL!
IT'S JUST A JOB TRANS-FER!!
WHO?!
BUT SOME KIDS ARE SAYING YOU WENT BANKRUPT ...
Keh.
Interrupting me.

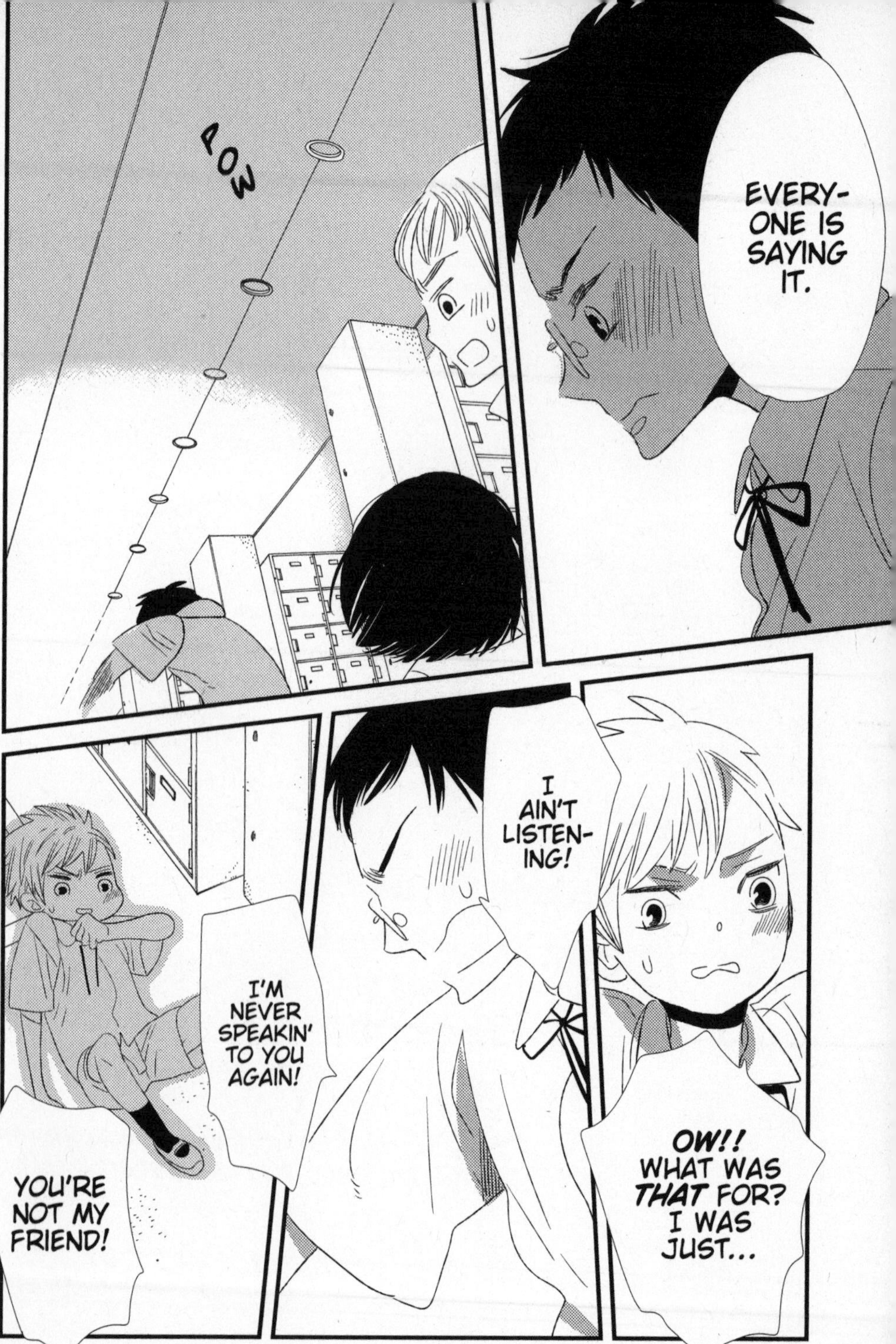
EVERY-ONE IS SAYING IT.
POW
OW!! WHAT WAS *THAT* FOR? I WAS JUST...
I AIN'T LISTEN-ING!
I'M NEVER SPEAKIN' TO YOU AGAIN!
YOU'RE NOT MY FRIEND!

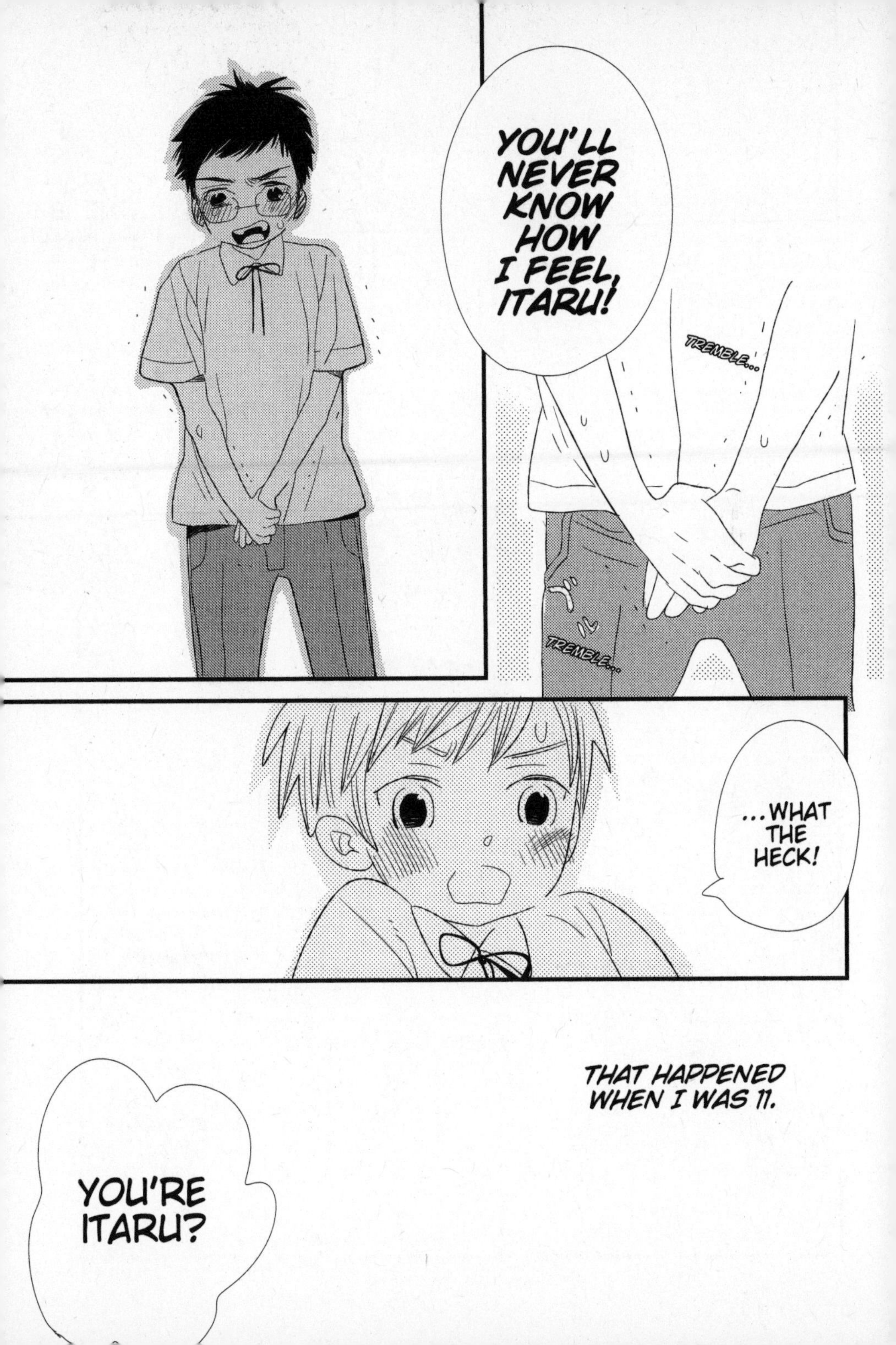
YOU'LL NEVER KNOW HOW I FEEL, ITARU!
TREMBLE...
TREMBLE...
...WHAT THE HECK!
THAT HAPPENED WHEN I WAS 11.
YOU'RE ITARU?

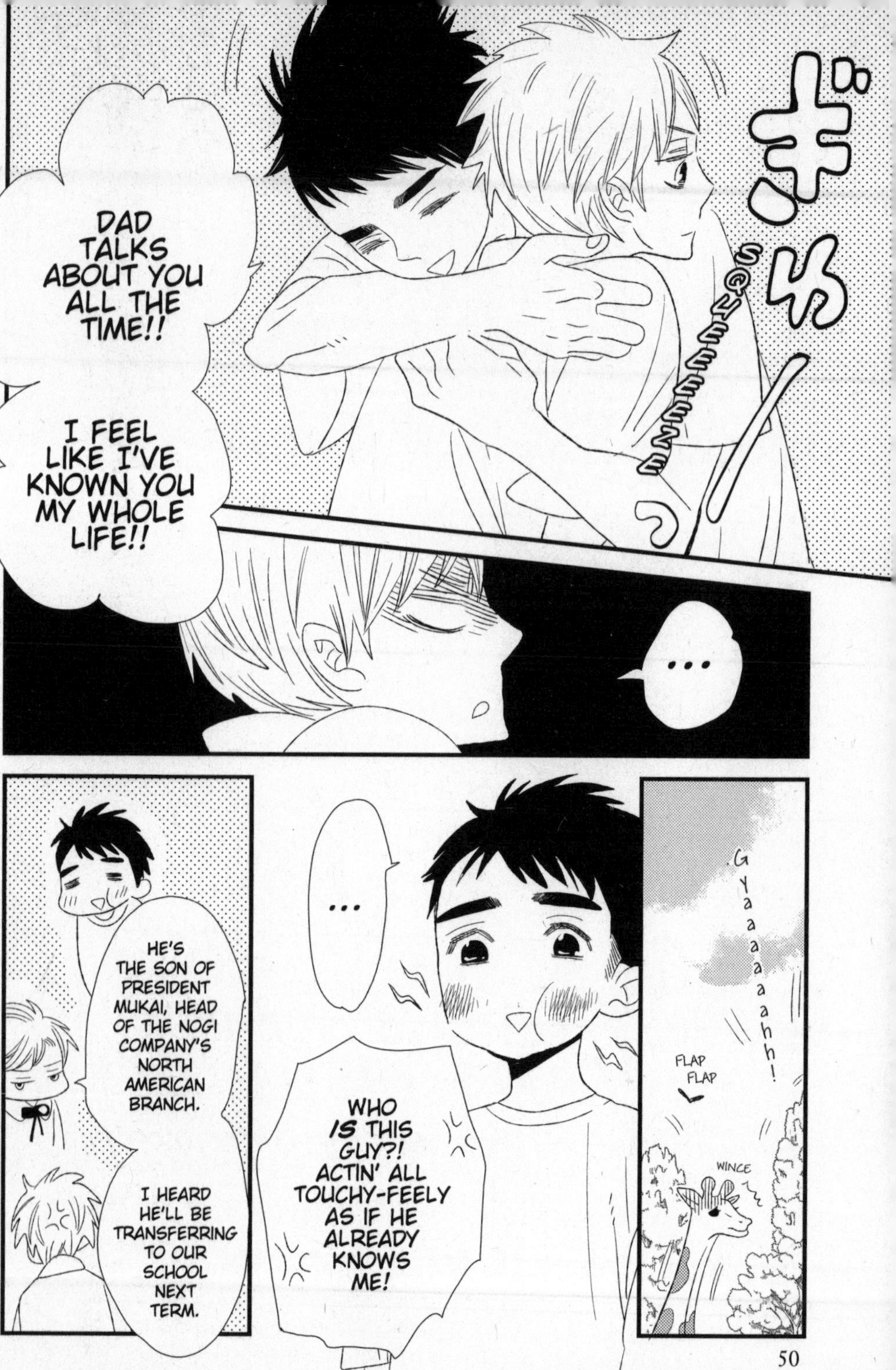
ぎゅっ
SQUEEEEEEZE
DAD TALKS ABOUT YOU ALL THE TIME!!
I FEEL LIKE I'VE KNOWN YOU MY WHOLE LIFE!!
...
Gyaaaaaahh!
FLAP FLAP
WINCE
...
WHO *IS* THIS GUY?! ACTIN' ALL TOUCHY-FEELY AS IF HE ALREADY KNOWS ME!
HE'S THE SON OF PRESIDENT MUKAI, HEAD OF THE NOGI COMPANY'S NORTH AMERICAN BRANCH.
I HEARD HE'LL BE TRANSFERRING TO OUR SCHOOL NEXT TERM.

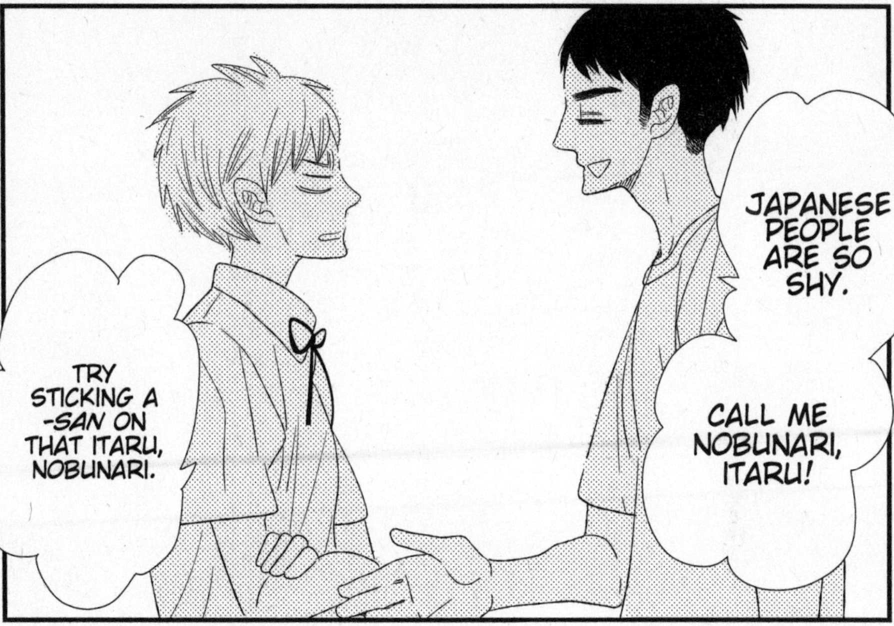
JAPANESE PEOPLE ARE SO SHY.
CALL ME NOBUNARI, ITARU!
TRY STICKING A -SAN ON THAT ITARU, NOBUNARI.

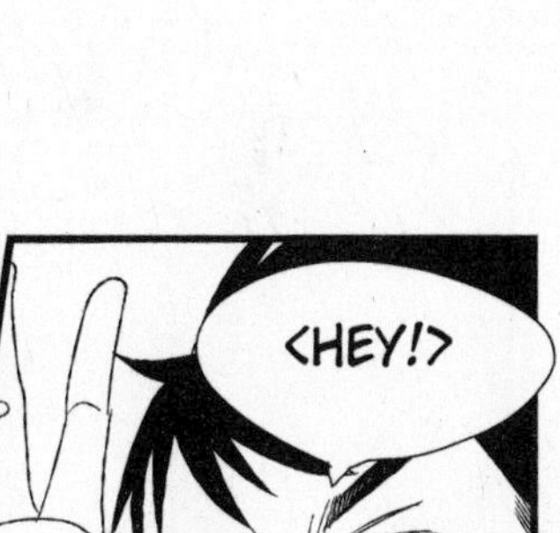
<HEY!>
<PASS IT OVER HERE! I'M OPEN!>

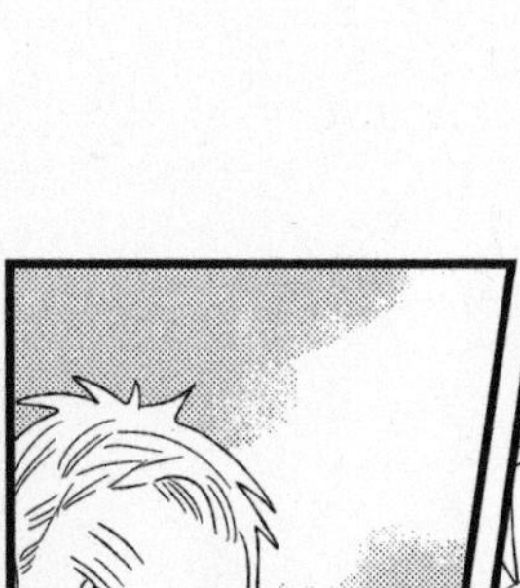

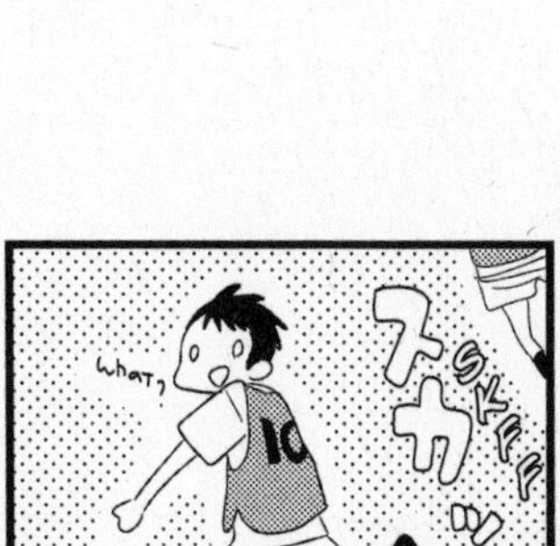
what,
SKFF
SKFF

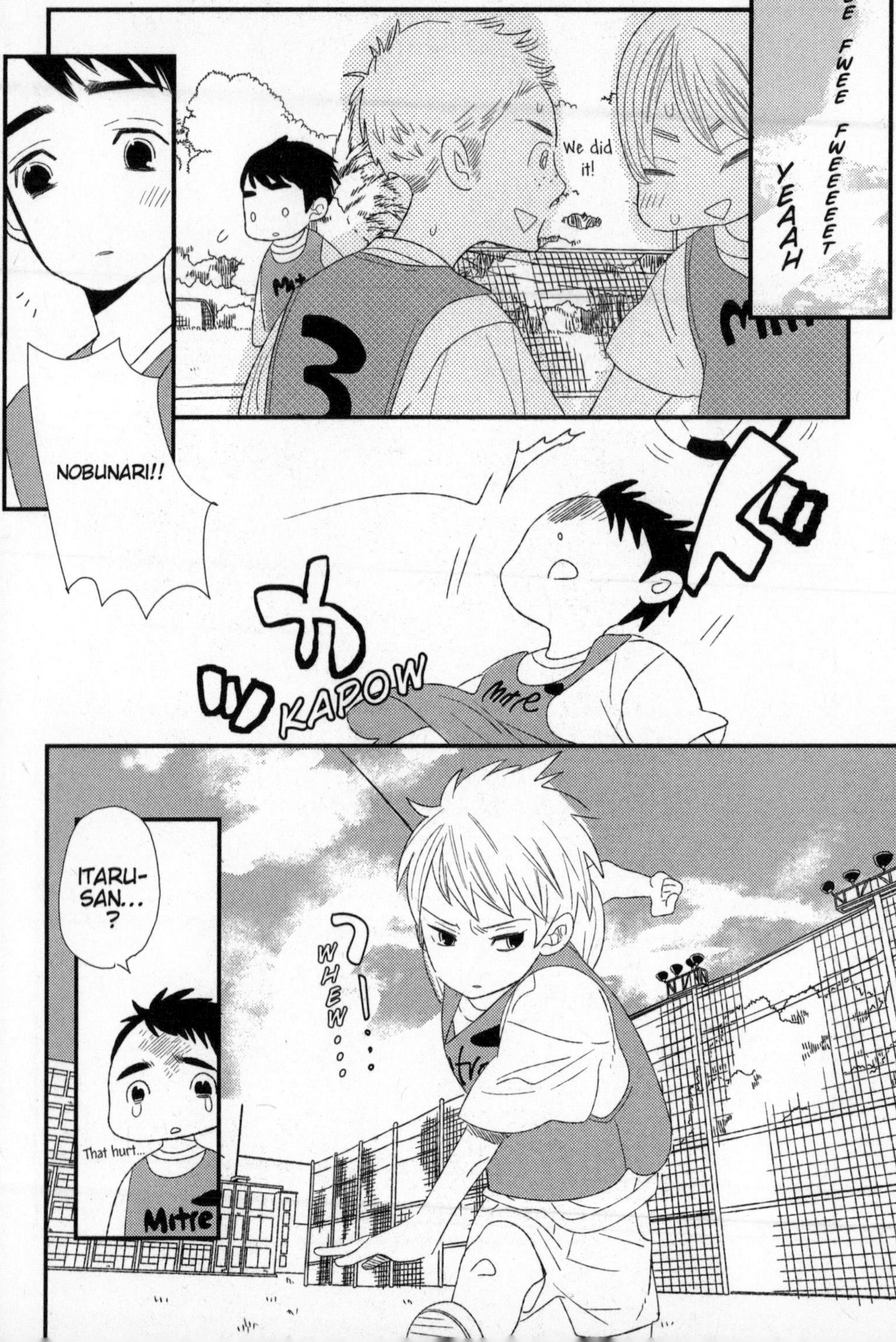
FWEE FWEE FWEEEEET
YEAAH
We did it!
NOBUNARI!!
KAPOW
ITARU-SAN...?
WHEW...
That hurt...

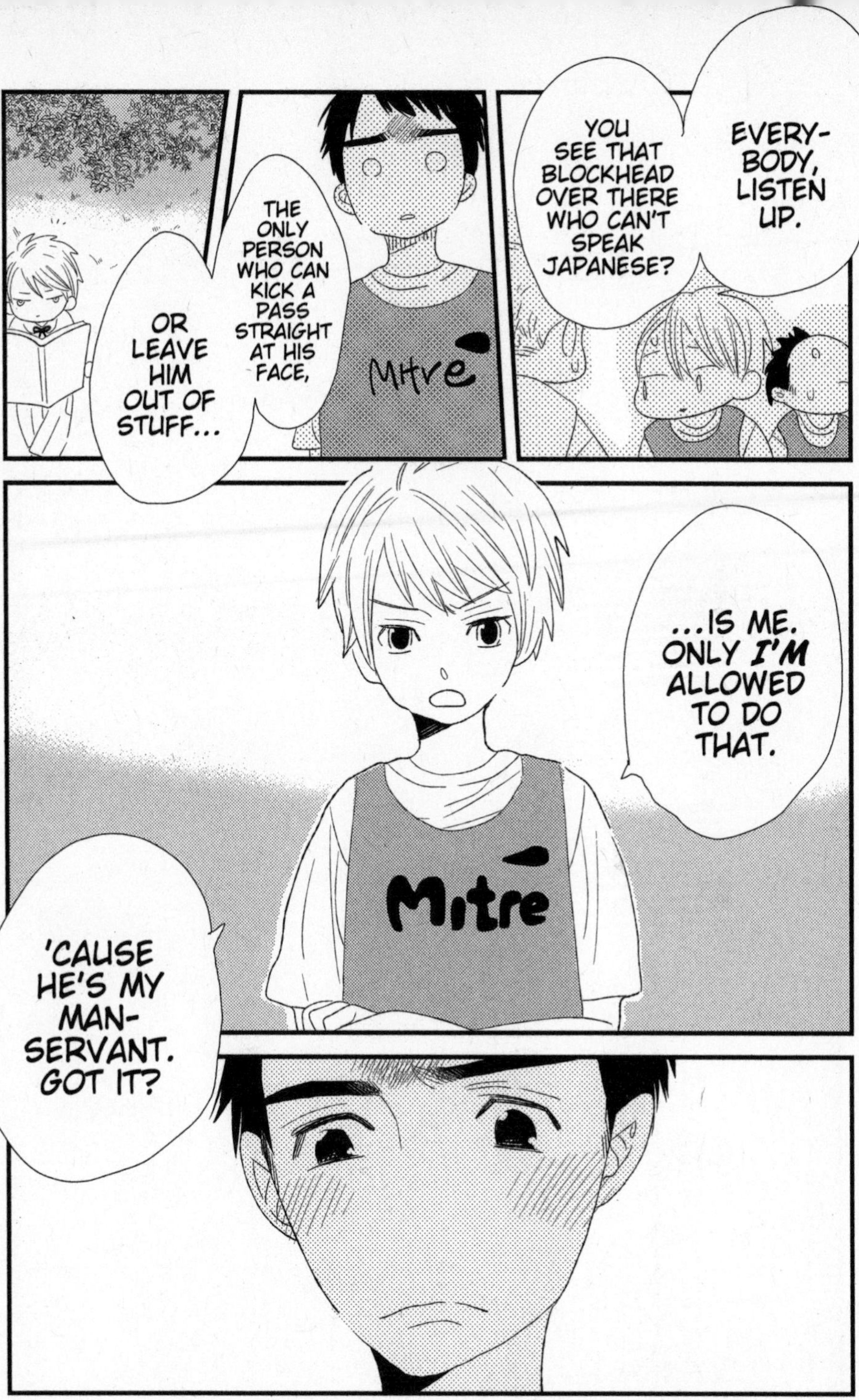
EVERY-BODY, LISTEN UP.
YOU SEE THAT BLOCKHEAD OVER THERE WHO CAN'T SPEAK JAPANESE?
Mitre
THE ONLY PERSON WHO CAN KICK A PASS STRAIGHT AT HIS FACE,
OR LEAVE HIM OUT OF STUFF...
...IS ME. ONLY *I'M* ALLOWED TO DO THAT.
Mitre
'CAUSE HE'S MY MAN-SERVANT. GOT IT?

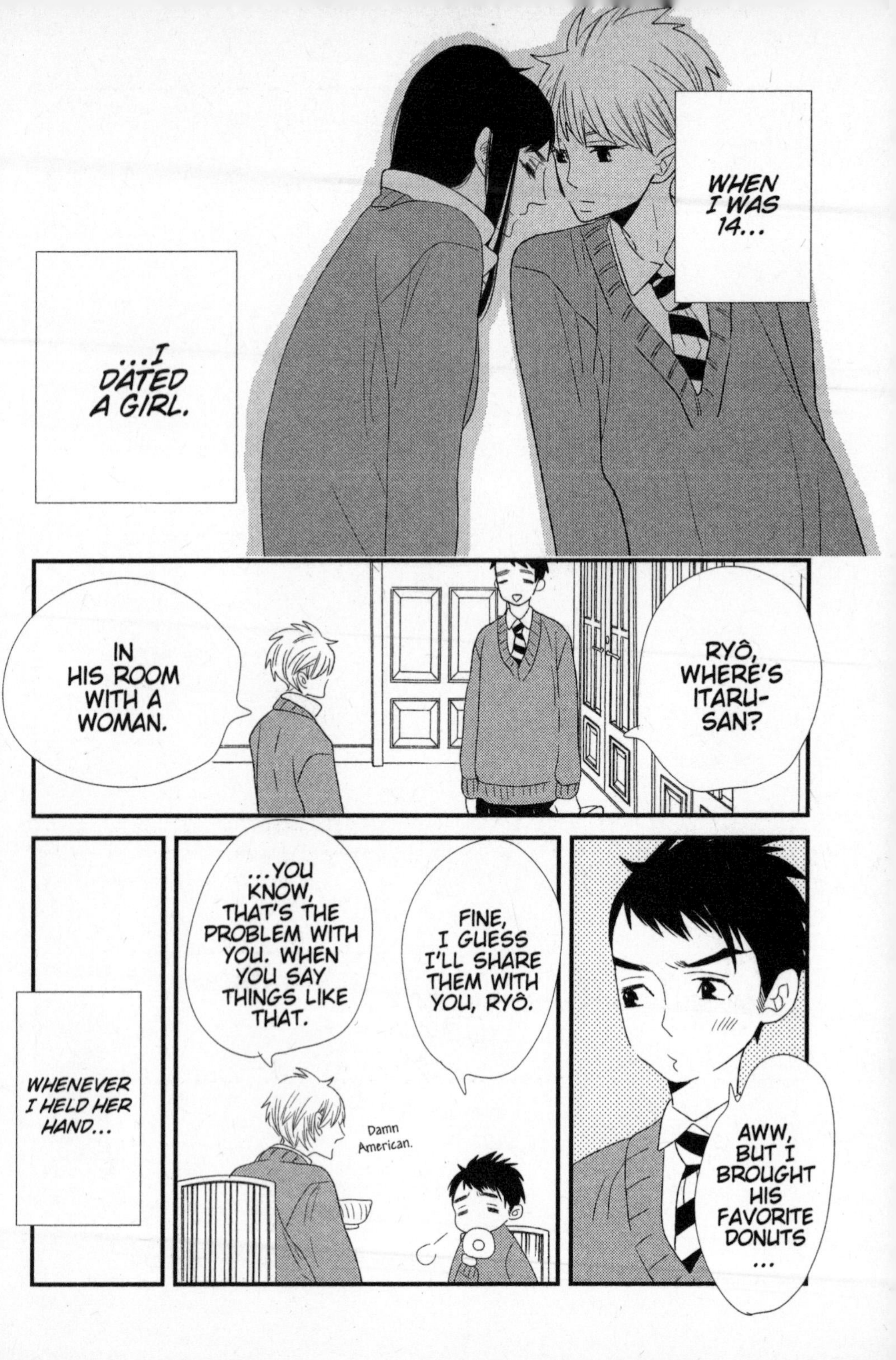
WHEN I WAS 14...
...I DATED A GIRL.
RYÔ, WHERE'S ITARU-SAN?
IN HIS ROOM WITH A WOMAN.
AWW, BUT I BROUGHT HIS FAVORITE DONUTS ...
FINE, I GUESS I'LL SHARE THEM WITH YOU, RYÔ.
...YOU KNOW, THAT'S THE PROBLEM WITH YOU. WHEN YOU SAY THINGS LIKE THAT.
Damn American.
WHENEVER I HELD HER HAND...

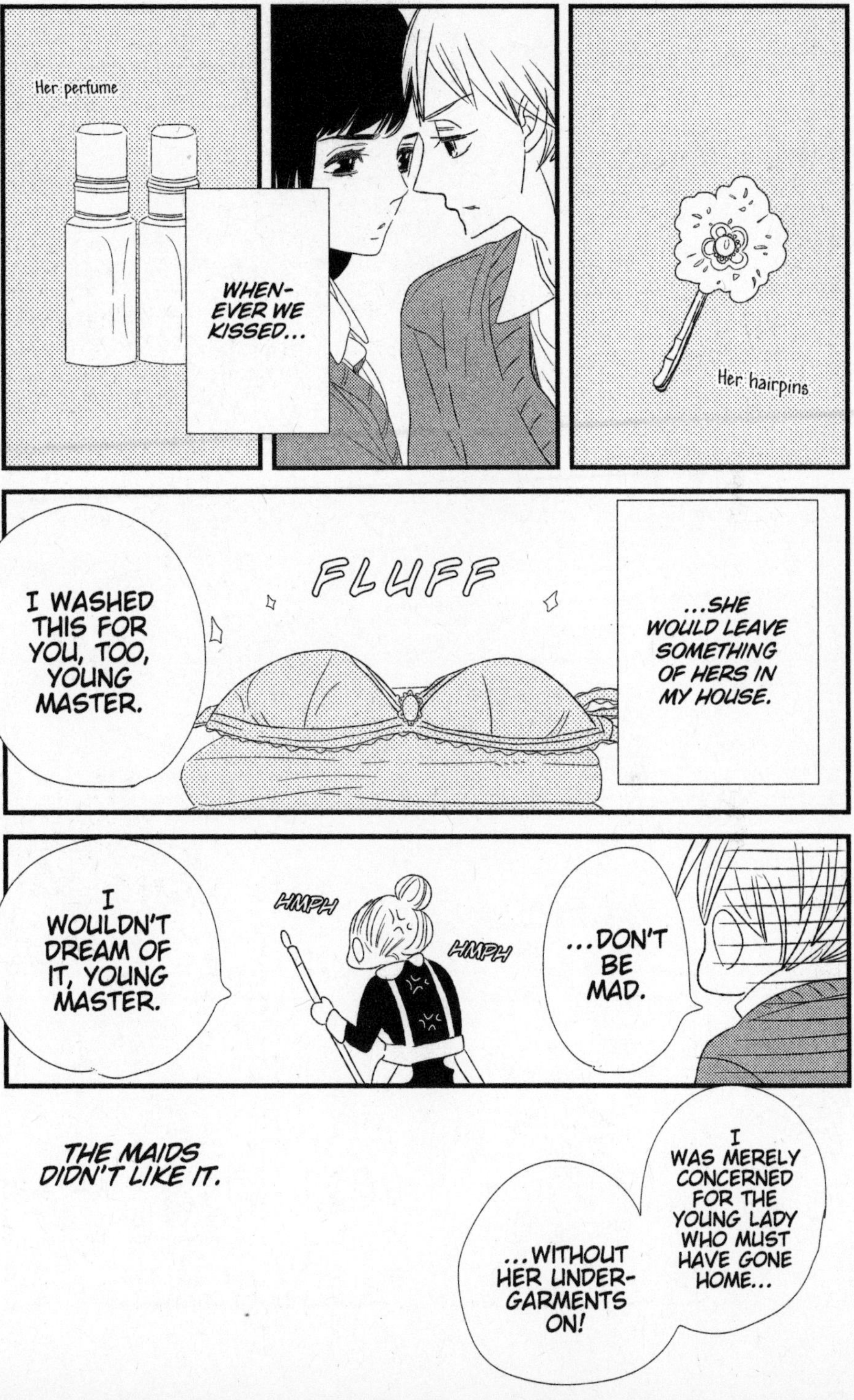
Her hairpins
WHEN-EVER WE KISSED...
Her perfume
...SHE WOULD LEAVE SOMETHING OF HERS IN MY HOUSE.
FLUFF
I WASHED THIS FOR YOU, TOO, YOUNG MASTER.
...DON'T BE MAD.
HMPH
HMPH
I WOULDN'T DREAM OF IT, YOUNG MASTER.
I WAS MERELY CONCERNED FOR THE YOUNG LADY WHO MUST HAVE GONE HOME...
...WITHOUT HER UNDER-GARMENTS ON!
THE MAIDS DIDN'T LIKE IT.

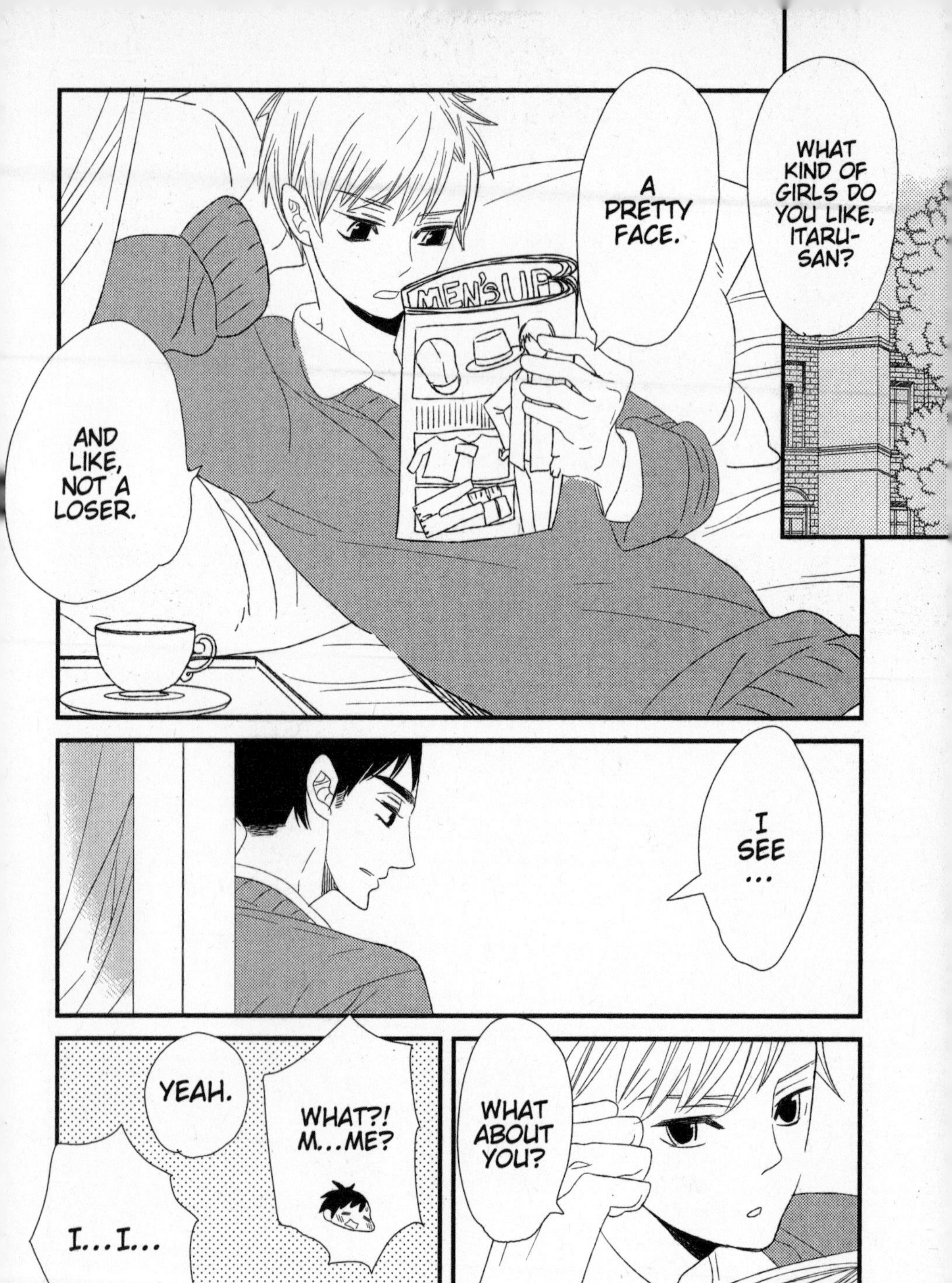
WHAT KIND OF GIRLS DO YOU LIKE, ITARU-SAN?
A PRETTY FACE.
AND LIKE, NOT A LOSER.
I SEE...
WHAT ABOUT YOU?
WHAT?! M...ME?
YEAH.
I...I...

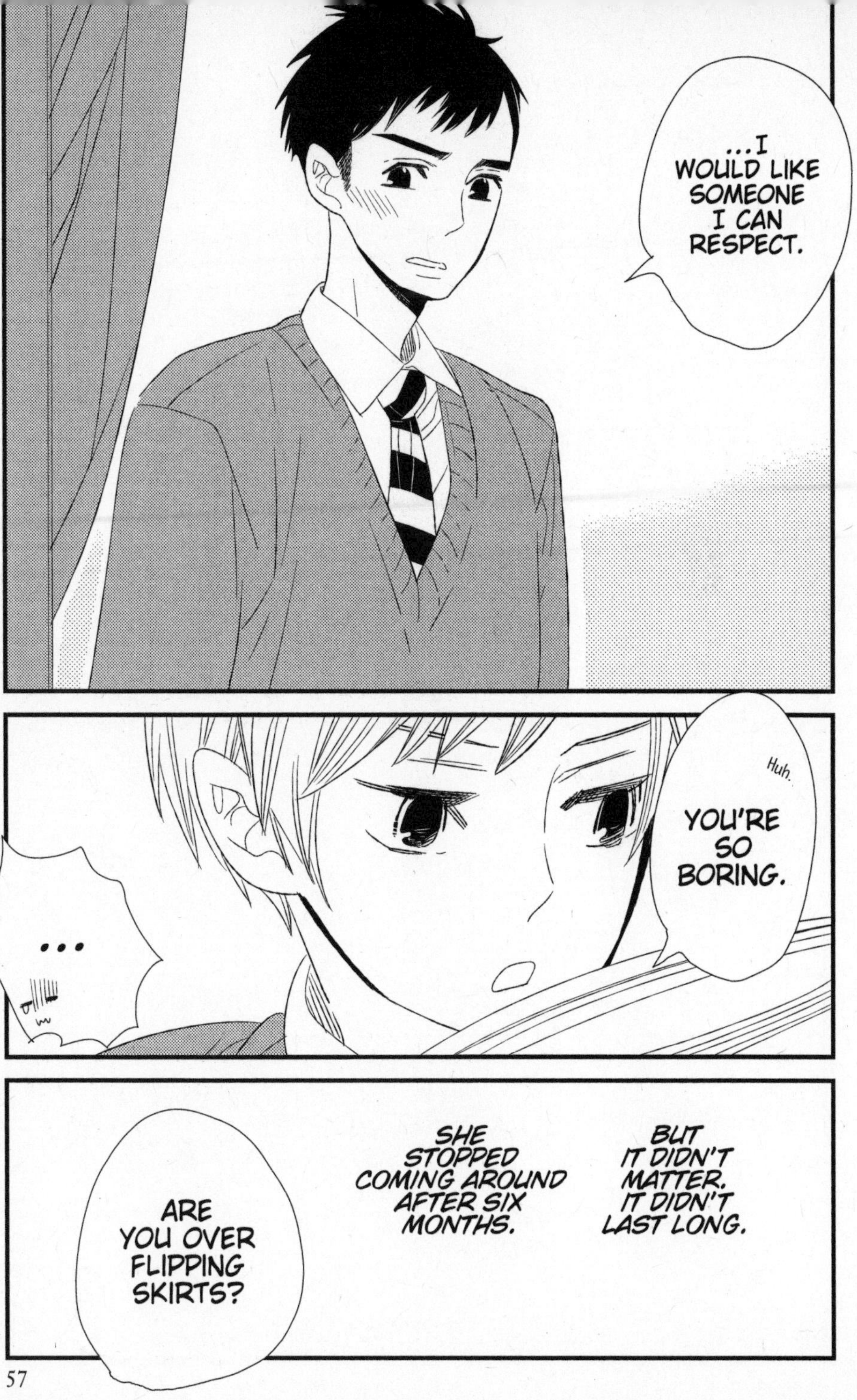
...I WOULD LIKE SOMEONE I CAN RESPECT.
Huh.
YOU'RE SO BORING.
...
BUT IT DIDN'T MATTER. IT DIDN'T LAST LONG.
SHE STOPPED COMING AROUND AFTER SIX MONTHS.
ARE YOU OVER FLIPPING SKIRTS?

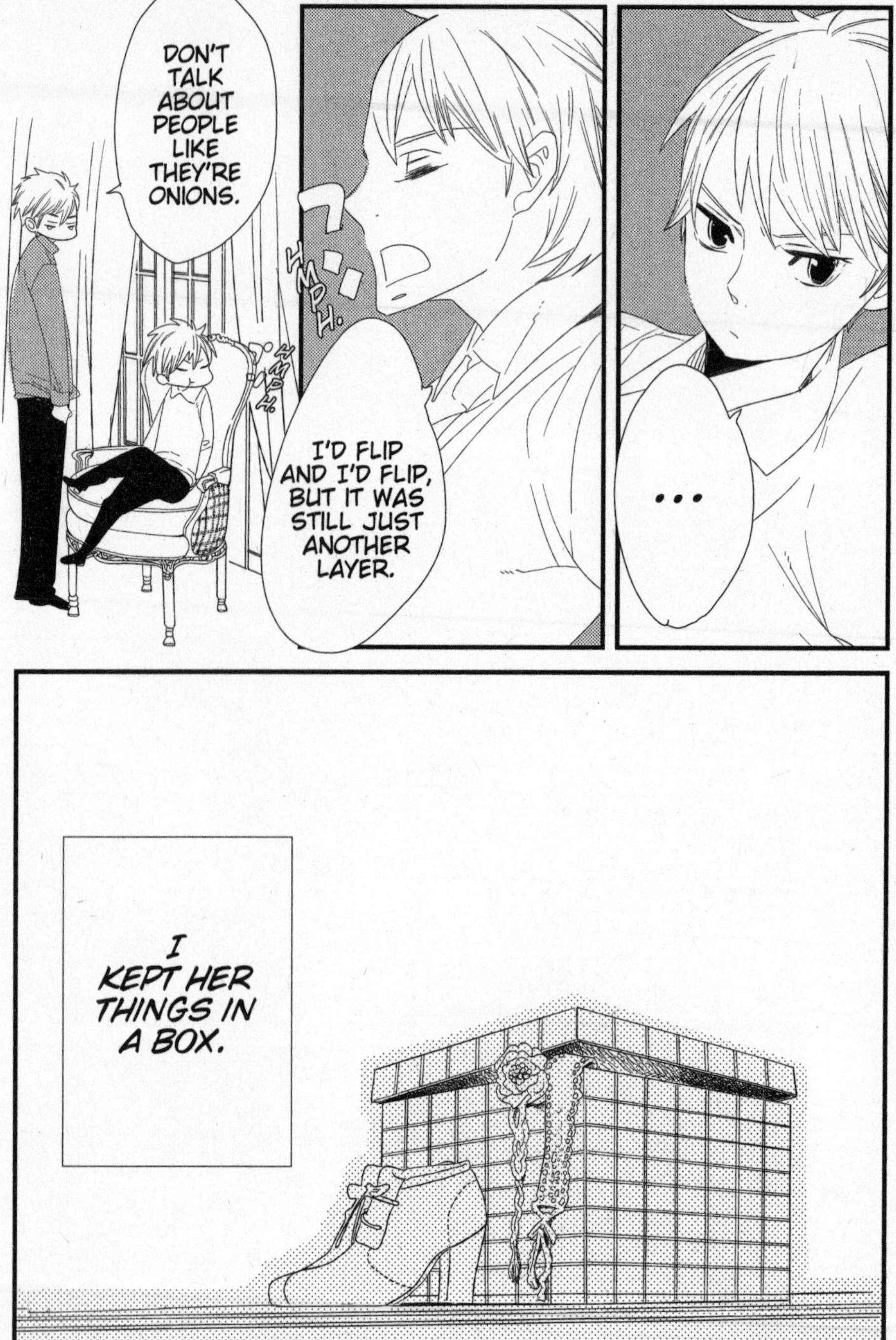
...
HMPH.
I'D FLIP AND I'D FLIP, BUT IT WAS STILL JUST ANOTHER LAYER.
DON'T TALK ABOUT PEOPLE LIKE THEY'RE ONIONS.
HMPH.
I KEPT HER THINGS IN A BOX.

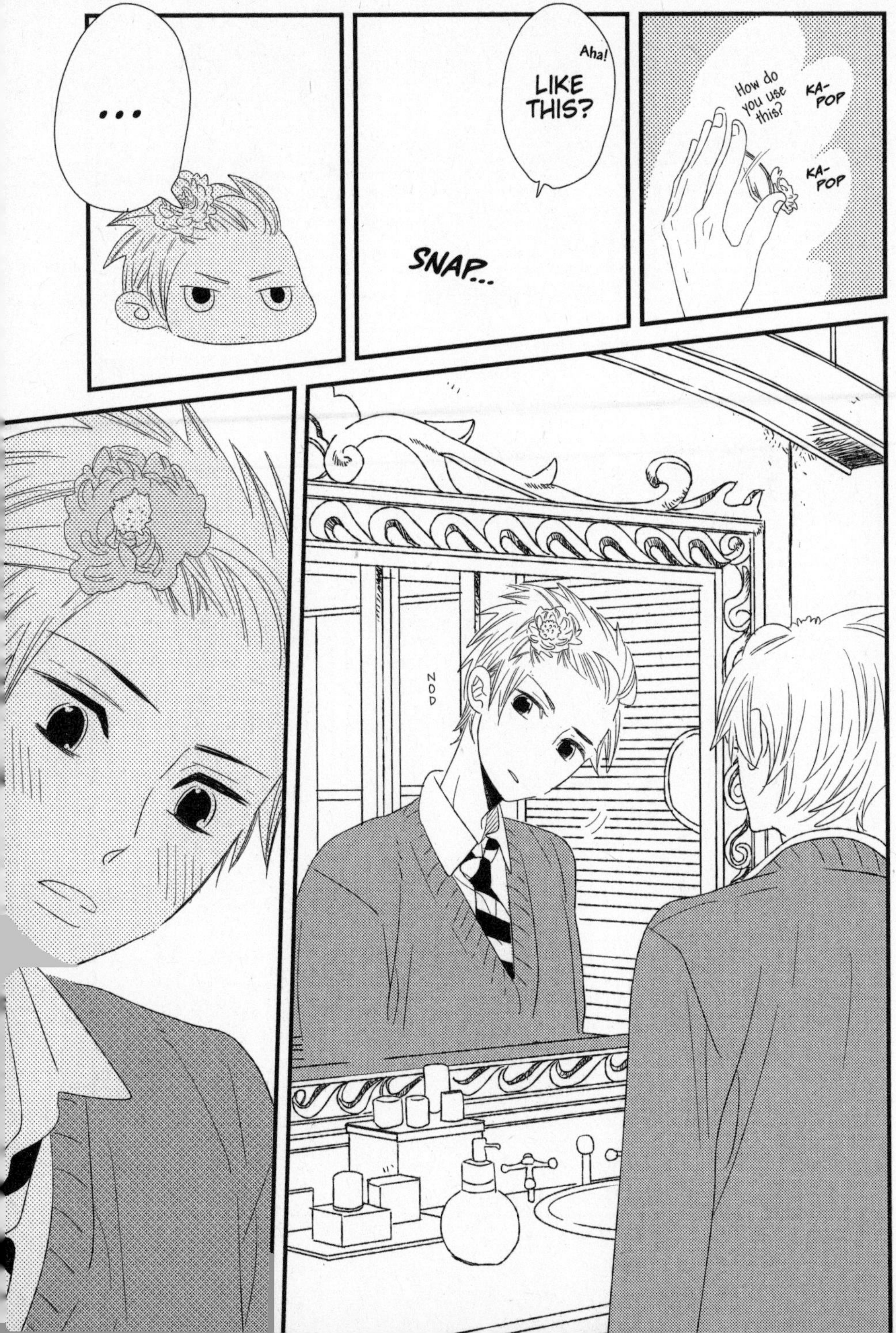
How do you use this?
KA-POP
KA-POP
Aha!
LIKE THIS?
SNAP...
...
NOD

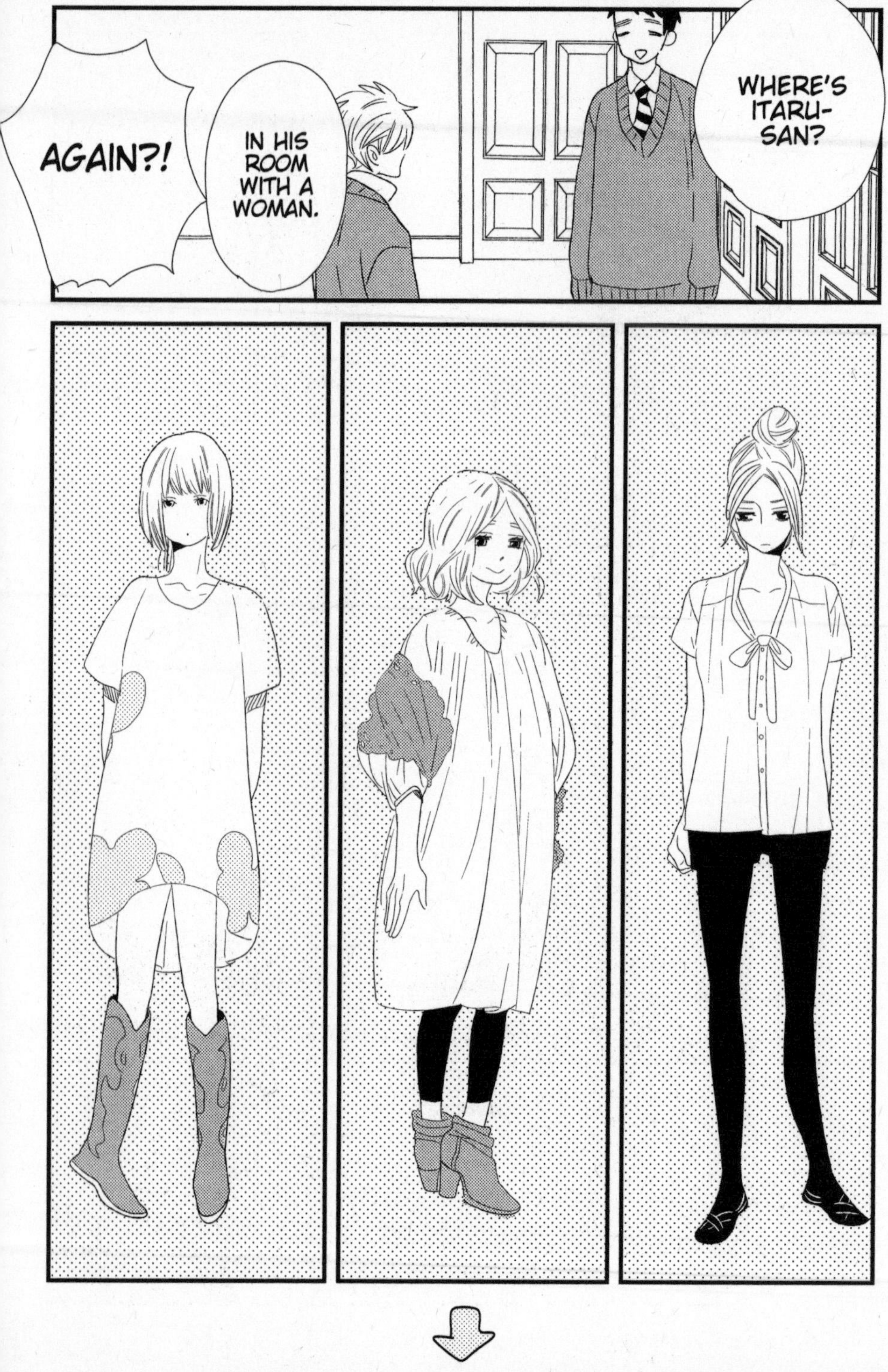
WHERE'S ITARU-SAN?
IN HIS ROOM WITH A WOMAN.
AGAIN?!

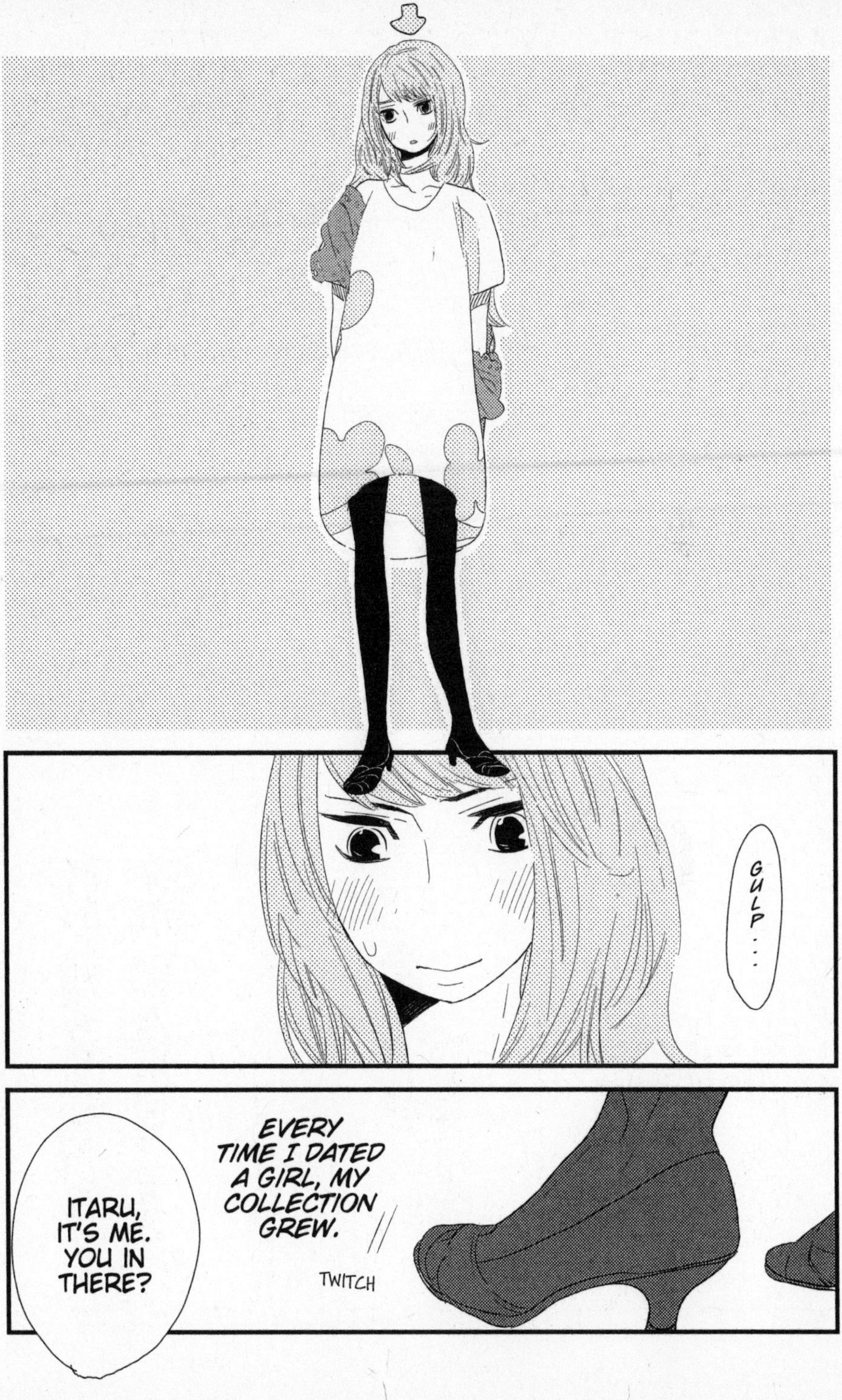
GULP...
EVERY TIME I DATED A GIRL, MY COLLECTION GREW.
TWITCH
ITARU, IT'S ME. YOU IN THERE?

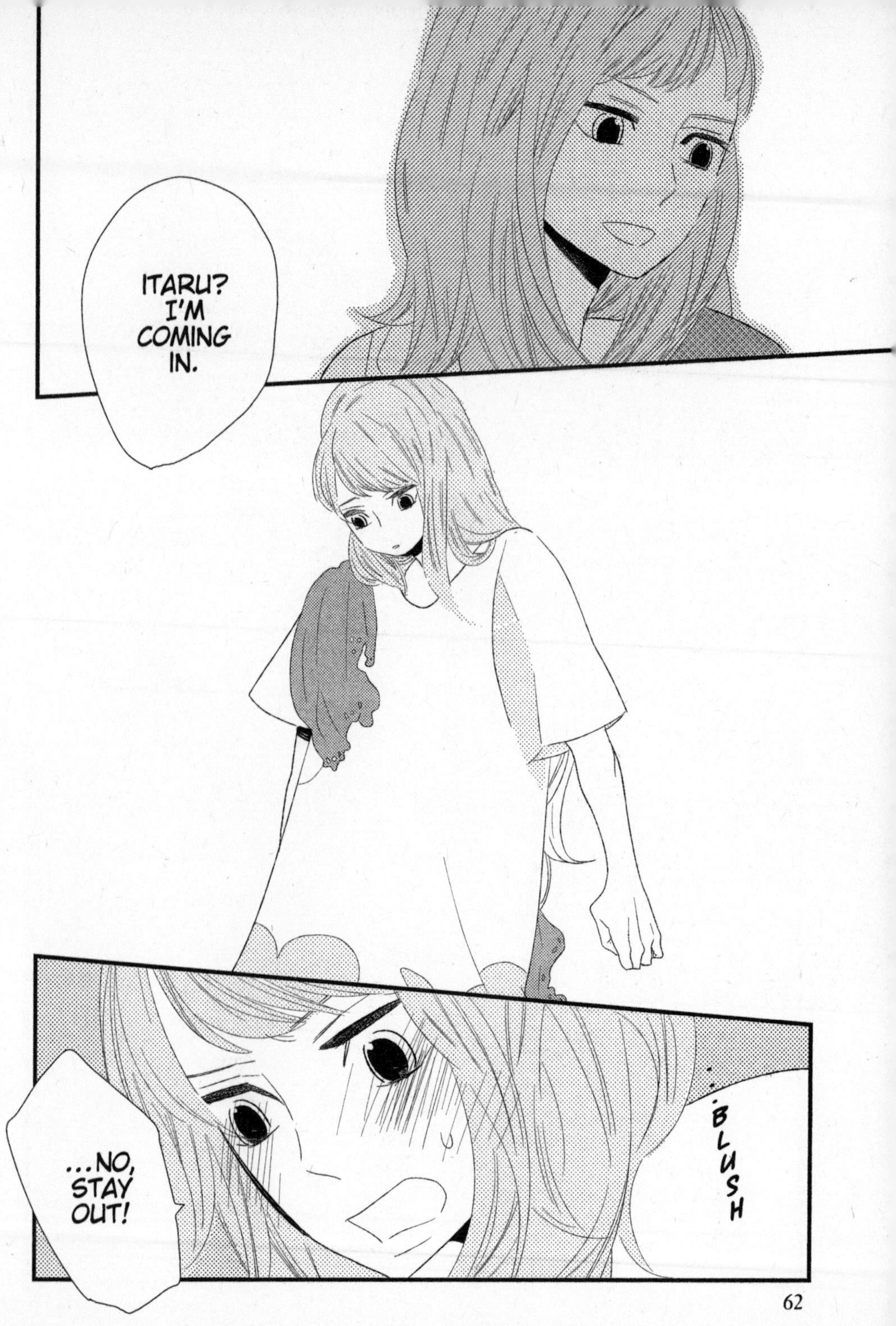
ITARU? I'M COMING IN.
...BLUSH
...NO, STAY OUT!

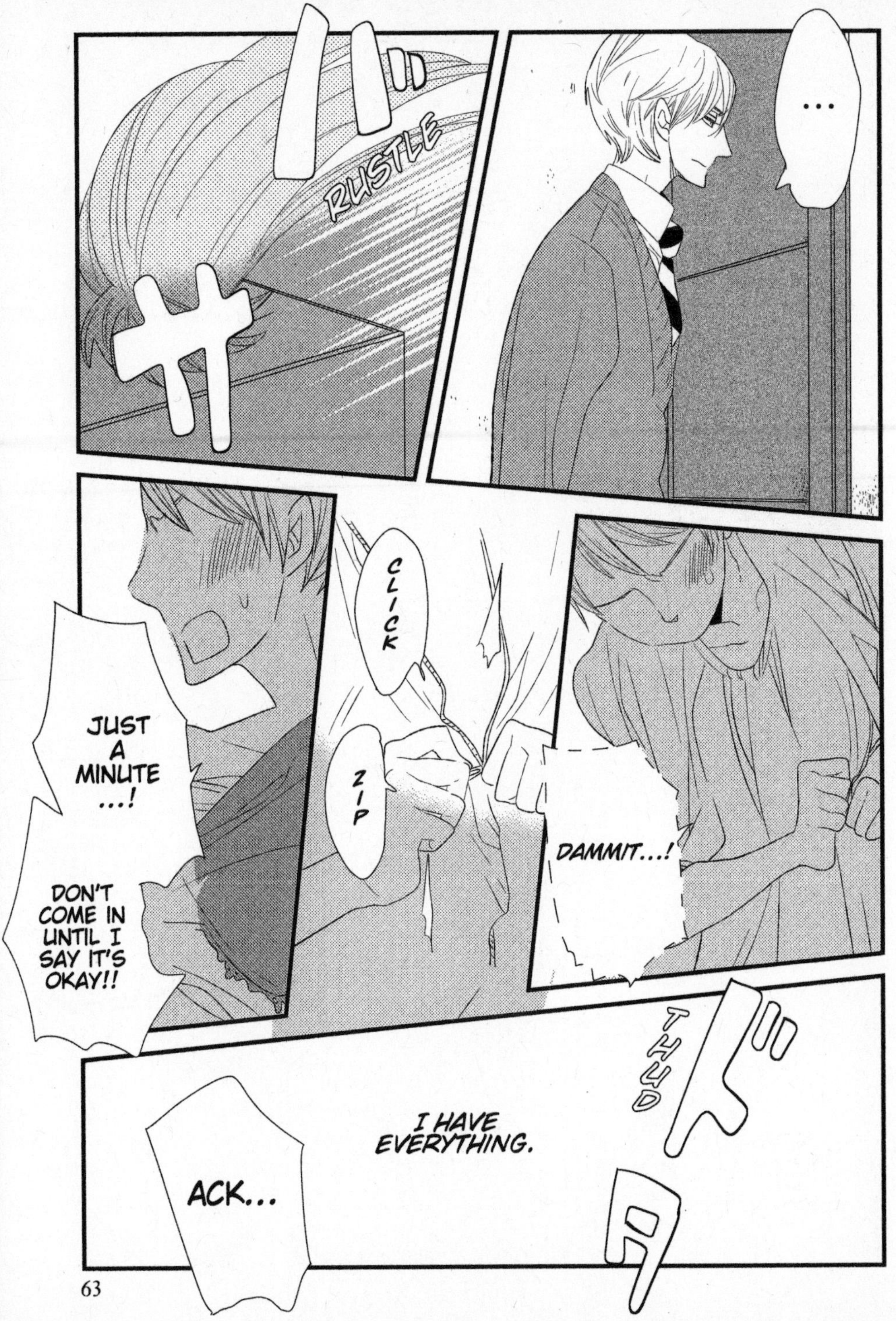
...
RUSTLE
DAMMIT...!
CLICK
ZIP
JUST A MINUTE...!
DON'T COME IN UNTIL I SAY IT'S OKAY!!
THUD
I HAVE EVERYTHING.
ACK...

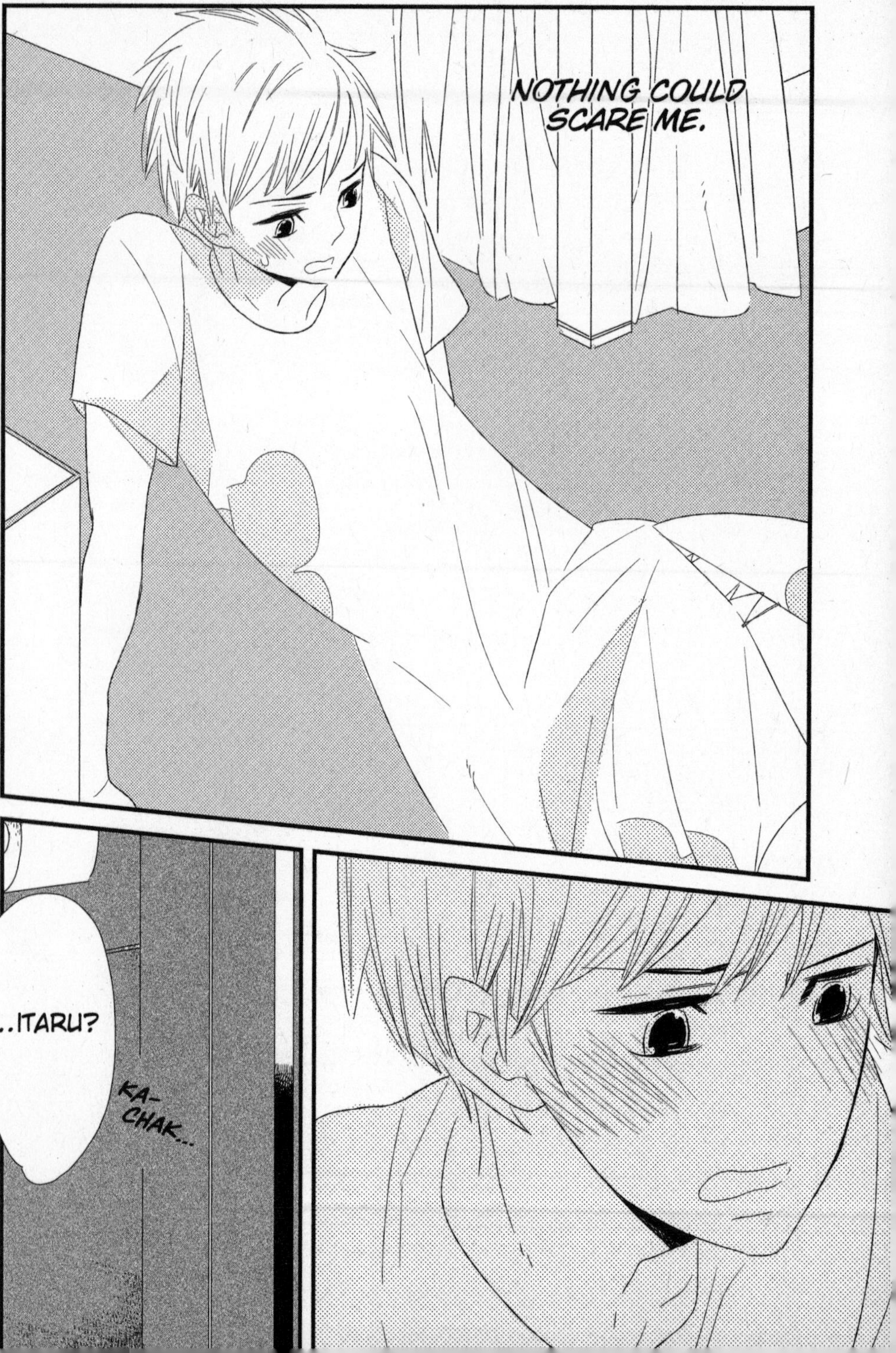
NOTHING COULD SCARE ME.
...ITARU?
KA-CHAK...

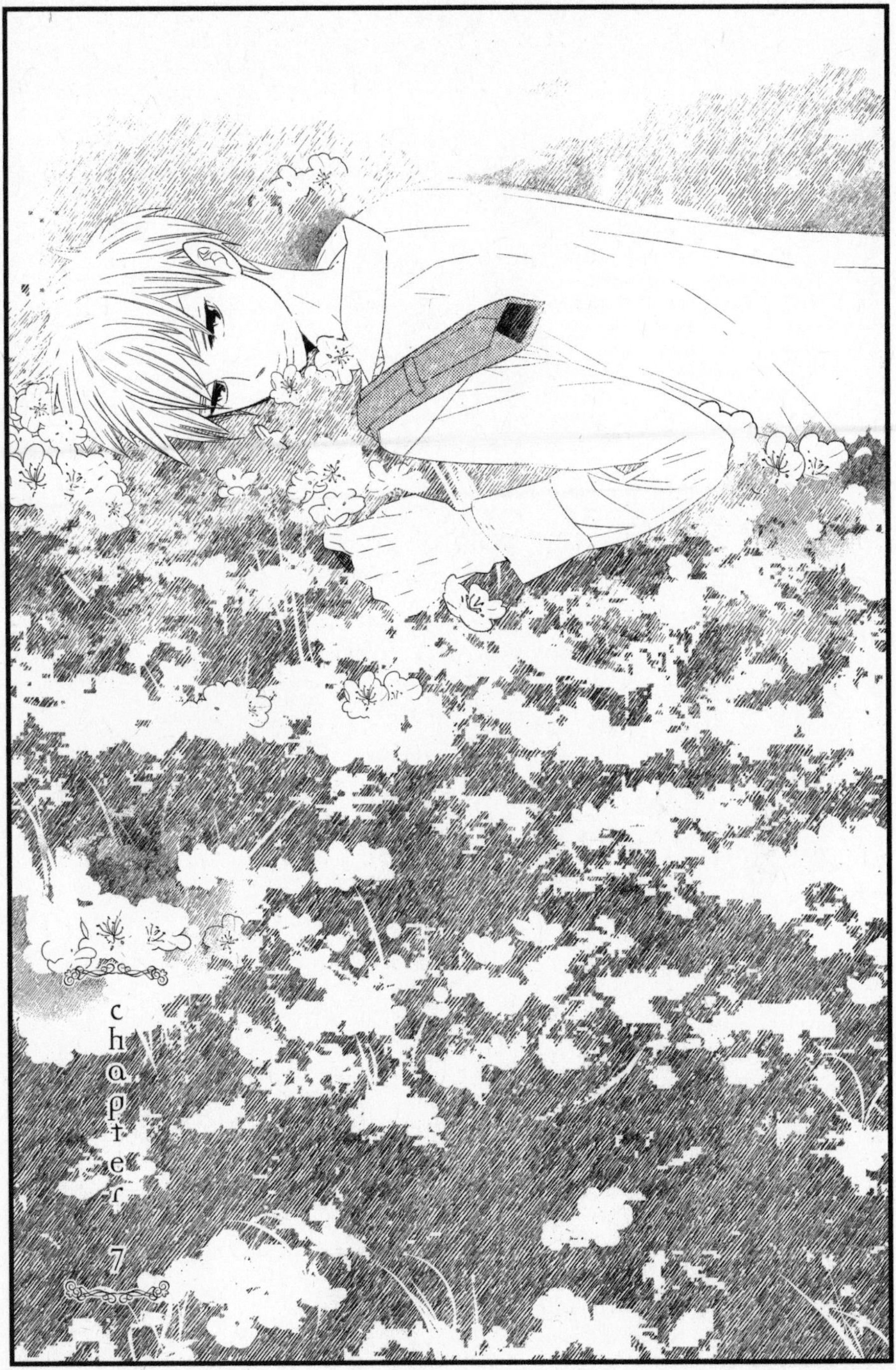
chapter 7

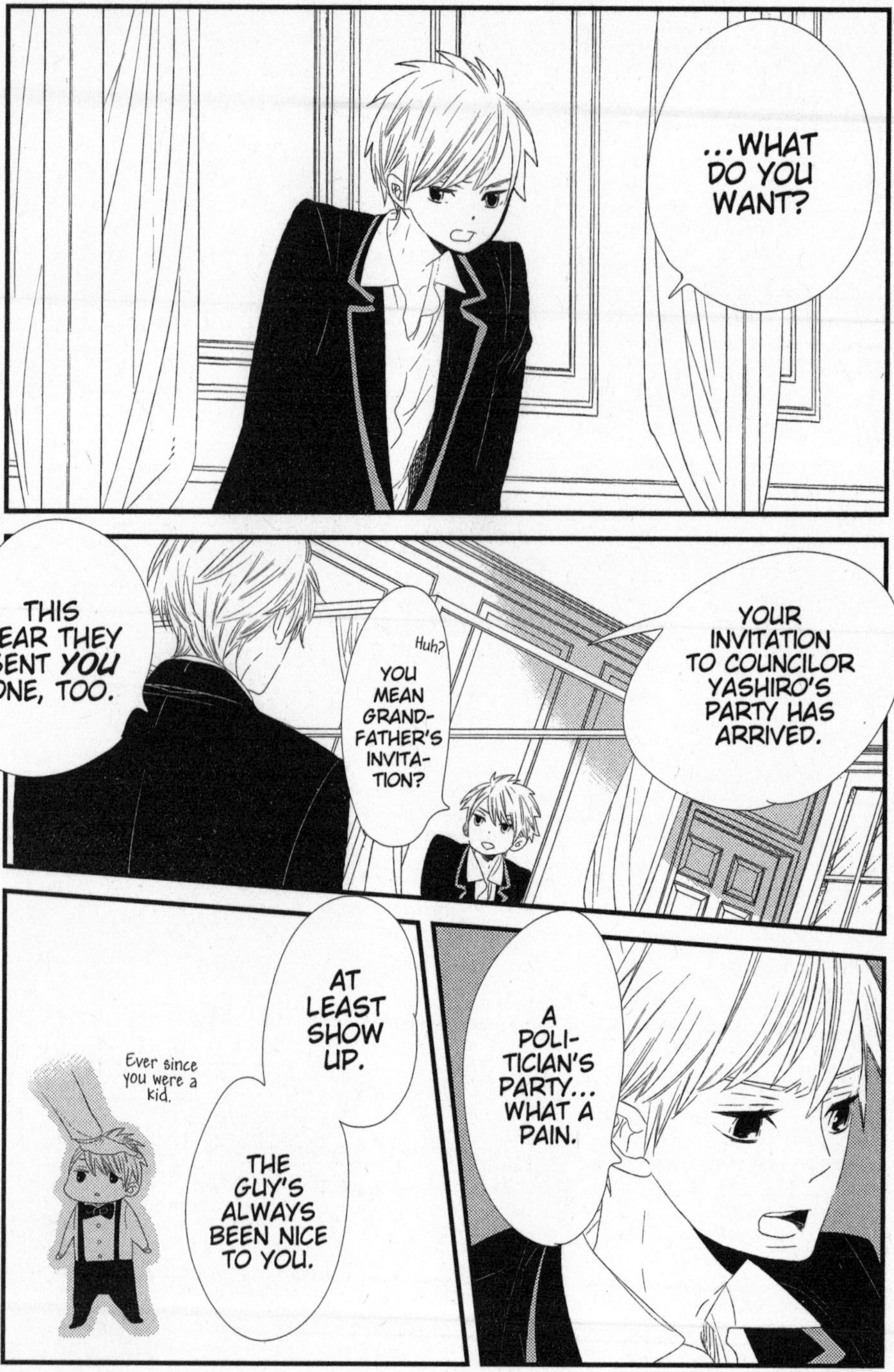

...WHAT DO YOU WANT?
YOUR INVITATION TO COUNCILOR YASHIRO'S PARTY HAS ARRIVED.
Huh?
YOU MEAN GRAND-FATHER'S INVITA-TION?
THIS YEAR THEY SENT *YOU* ONE, TOO.
A POLI-TICIAN'S PARTY... WHAT A PAIN.
AT LEAST SHOW UP.
THE GUY'S ALWAYS BEEN NICE TO YOU.
Ever since you were a kid.

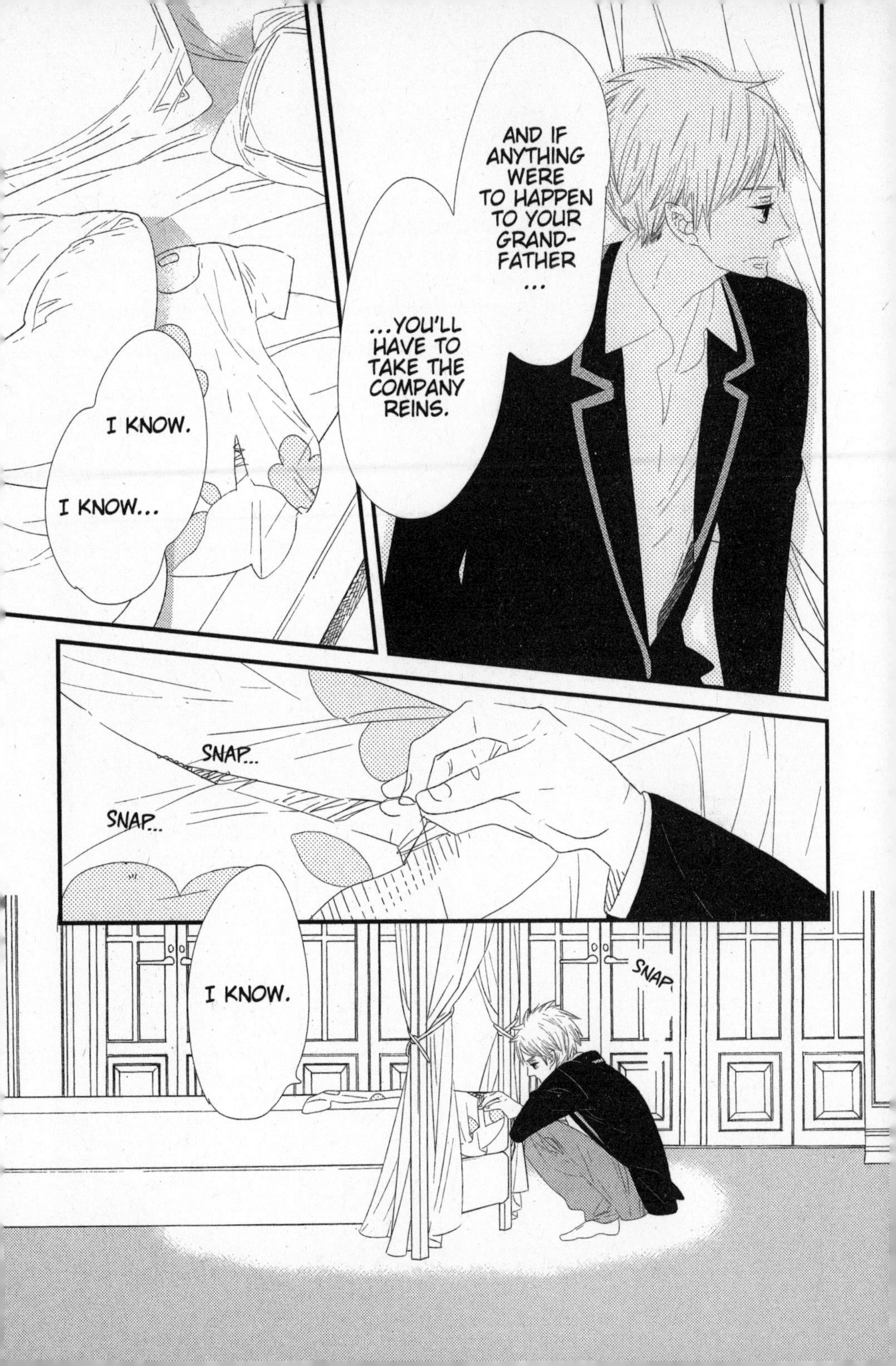
AND IF ANYTHING WERE TO HAPPEN TO YOUR GRAND-FATHER ...
...YOU'LL HAVE TO TAKE THE COMPANY REINS.
I KNOW.
I KNOW...
SNAP...
SNAP...
SNAP
I KNOW.

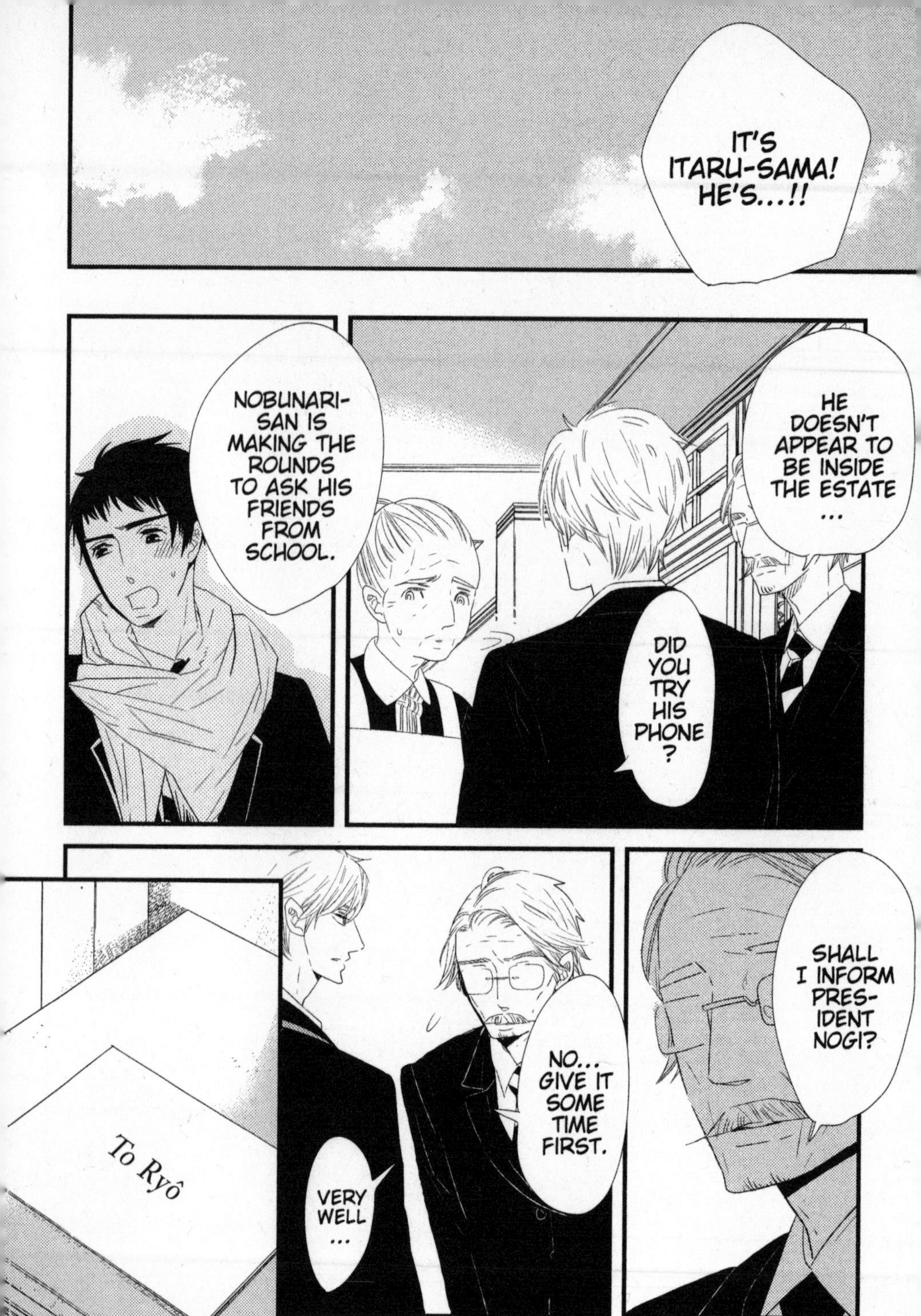
IT'S ITARU-SAMA! HE'S...!!
HE DOESN'T APPEAR TO BE INSIDE THE ESTATE...
DID YOU TRY HIS PHONE?
NOBUNARI-SAN IS MAKING THE ROUNDS TO ASK HIS FRIENDS FROM SCHOOL.
SHALL I INFORM PRES-IDENT NOGI?
NO... GIVE IT SOME TIME FIRST.
VERY WELL...
To Ryô

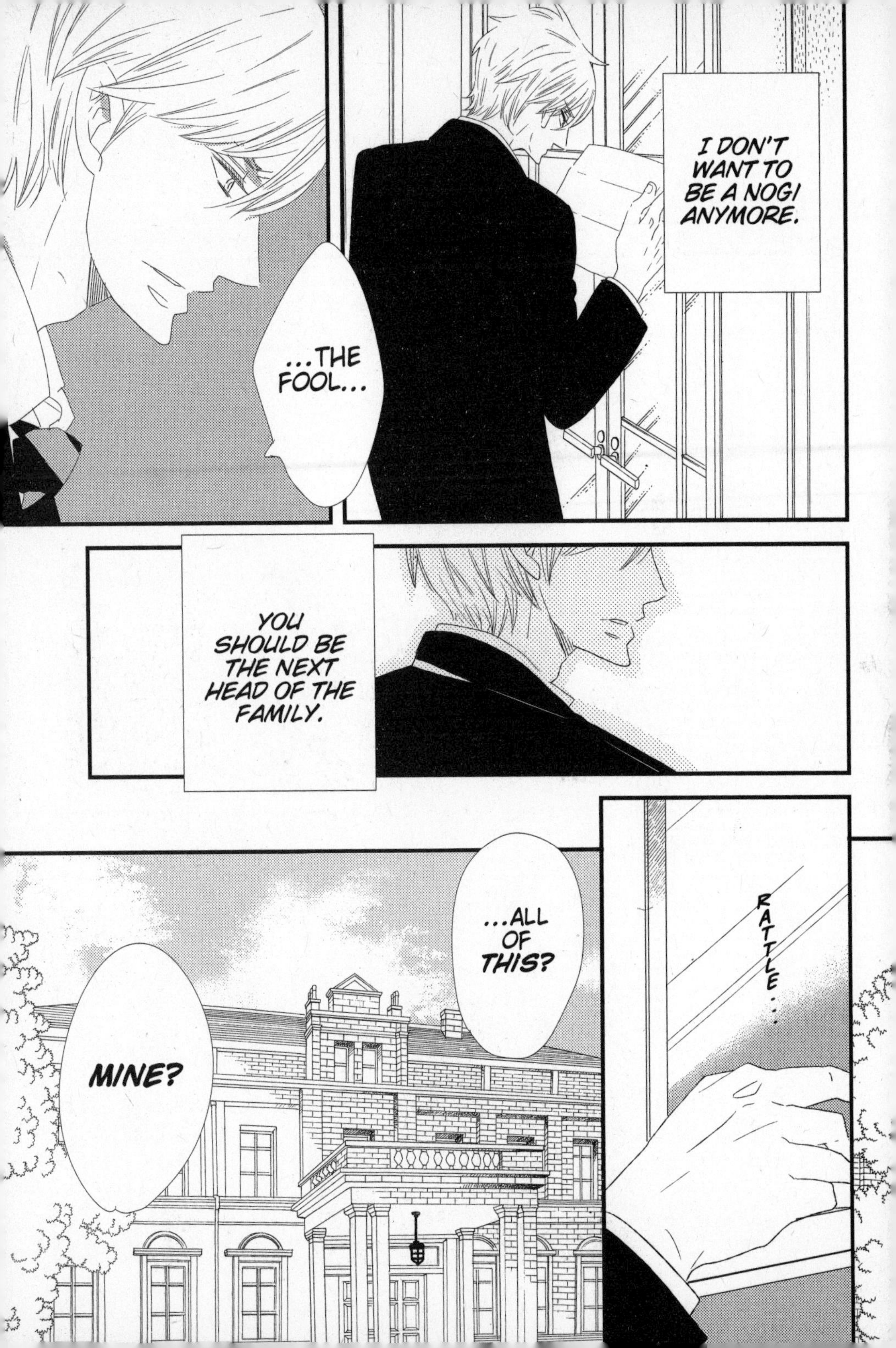
I DON'T WANT TO BE A NOGI ANYMORE.
...THE FOOL...
YOU SHOULD BE THE NEXT HEAD OF THE FAMILY.
RATTLE...
...ALL OF THIS?
MINE?

70

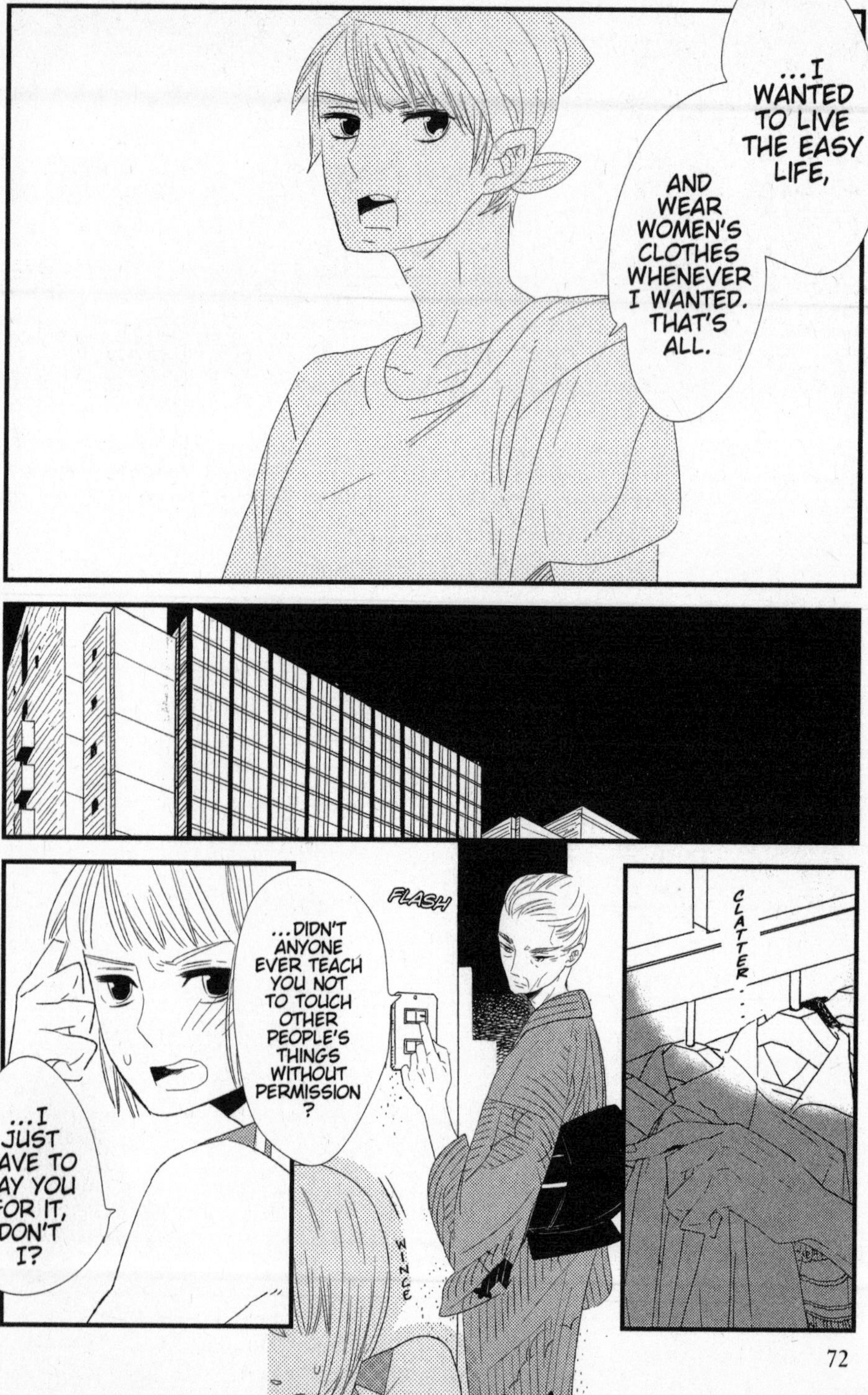
...I WANTED TO LIVE THE EASY LIFE,
AND WEAR WOMEN'S CLOTHES WHENEVER I WANTED. THAT'S ALL.
CLATTER...
FLASH
...DIDN'T ANYONE EVER TEACH YOU NOT TO TOUCH OTHER PEOPLE'S THINGS WITHOUT PERMISSION?
...I JUST HAVE TO PAY YOU FOR IT, DON'T I?
WINCE

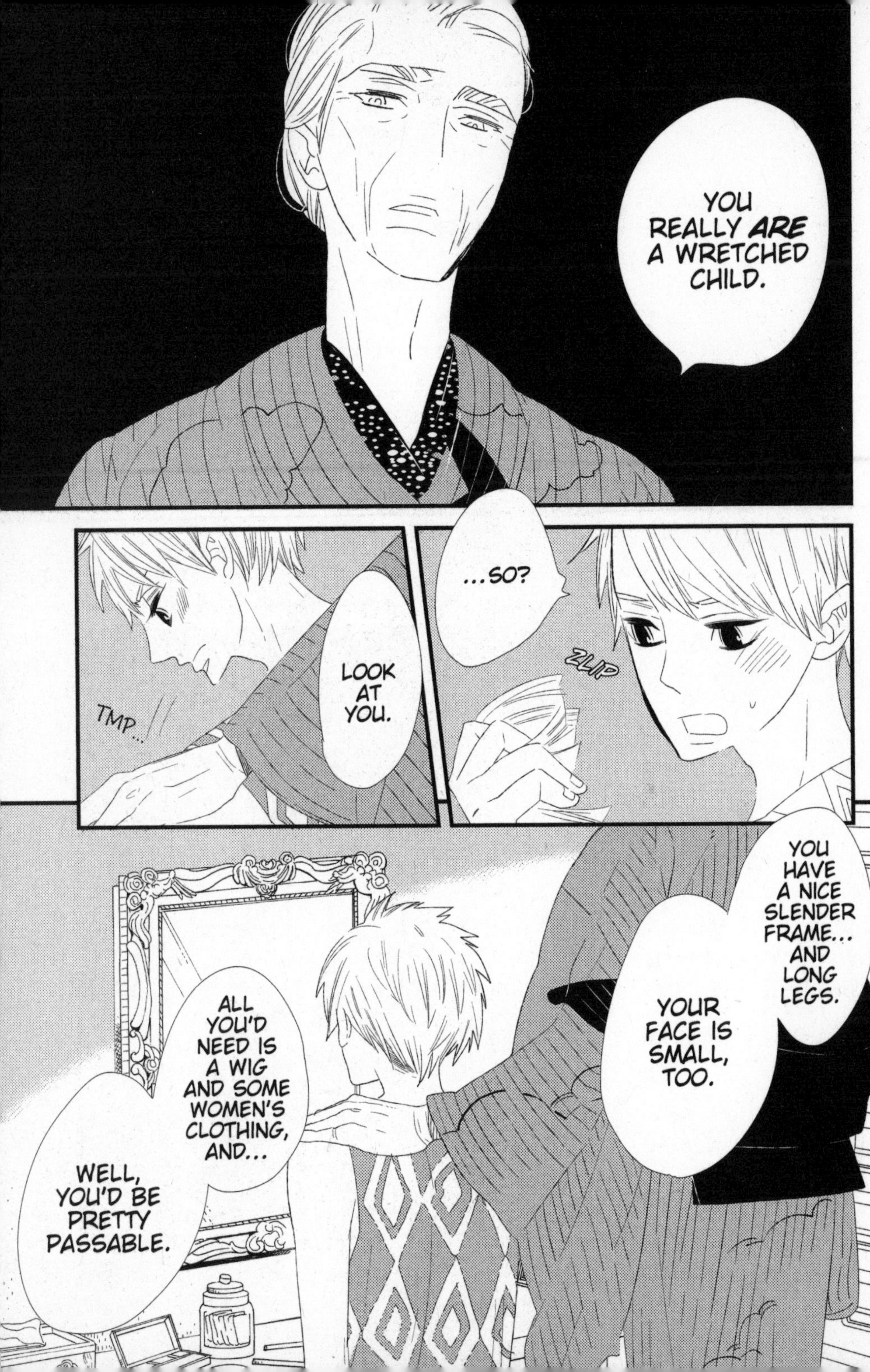
YOU REALLY ARE A WRETCHED CHILD.
...SO?
ZLIP
LOOK AT YOU.
TMP...
YOU HAVE A NICE SLENDER FRAME... AND LONG LEGS.
YOUR FACE IS SMALL, TOO.
ALL YOU'D NEED IS A WIG AND SOME WOMEN'S CLOTHING, AND...
WELL, YOU'D BE PRETTY PASSABLE.

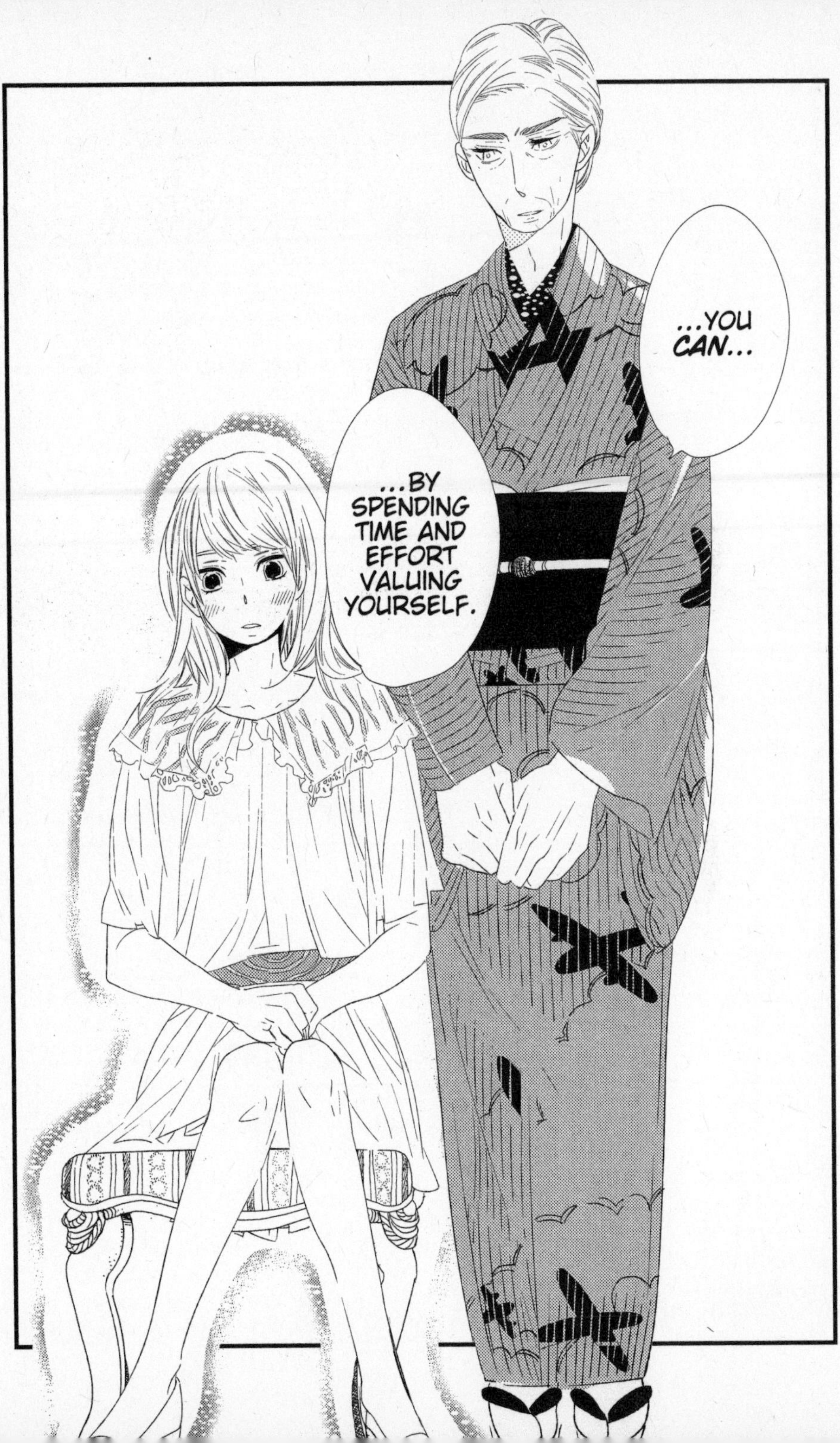
...YOU CAN...
...BY SPENDING TIME AND EFFORT VALUING YOURSELF.

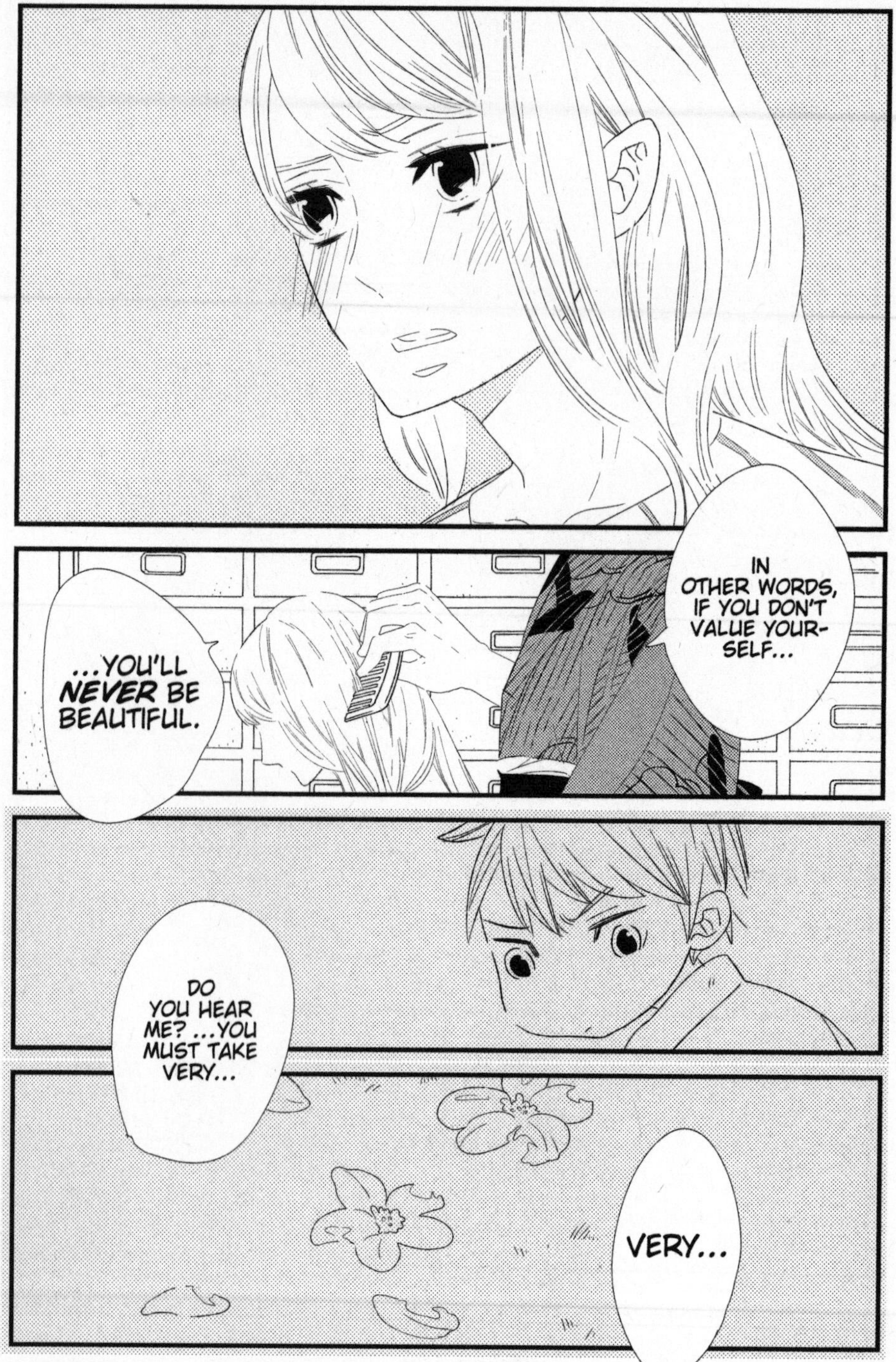
IN OTHER WORDS, IF YOU DON'T VALUE YOUR-SELF...
...YOU'LL **NEVER** BE BEAUTIFUL.
DO YOU HEAR ME? ...YOU MUST TAKE VERY...
VERY...

78

DRINK SOME TEA!

...

Here.

HAVE SOME SNACKS.

I PUT ONE BOX ON A SHELF AND THEY'RE JUMPING FOR JOY.

WHAT IS WITH THESE GUYS...?

Oh, my, Maki-chan! That's the good green tea!

Your Bunmeido dorayaki is delicious, too, Miki-chan! ♡

IS THAT REALLY ALL I HAVE TO DO?

...WHAT'S UP WITH THAT?

MUNCH

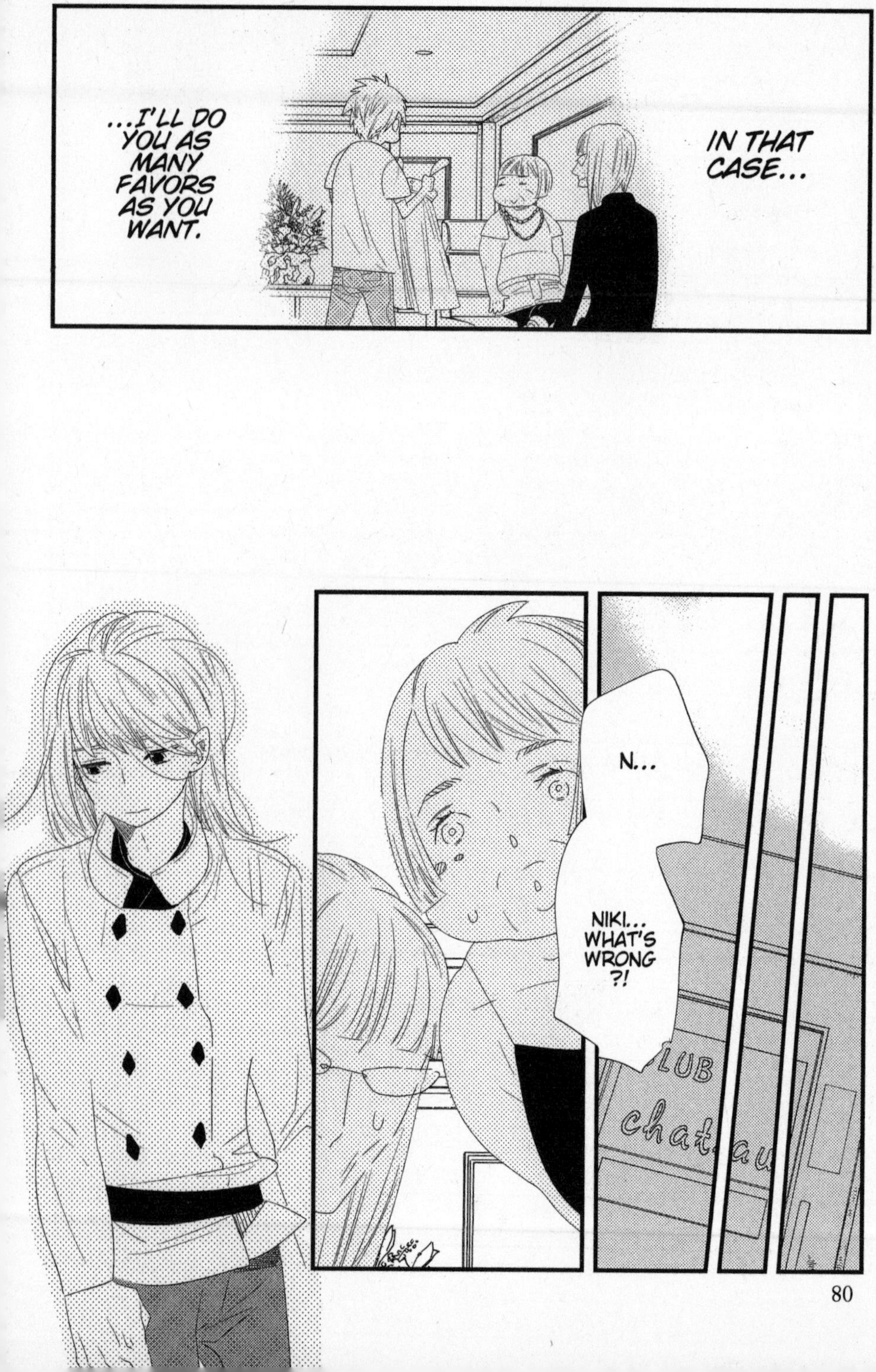
IN THAT CASE...
...I'LL DO YOU AS MANY FAVORS AS YOU WANT.
N...
NIKI... WHAT'S WRONG ?!

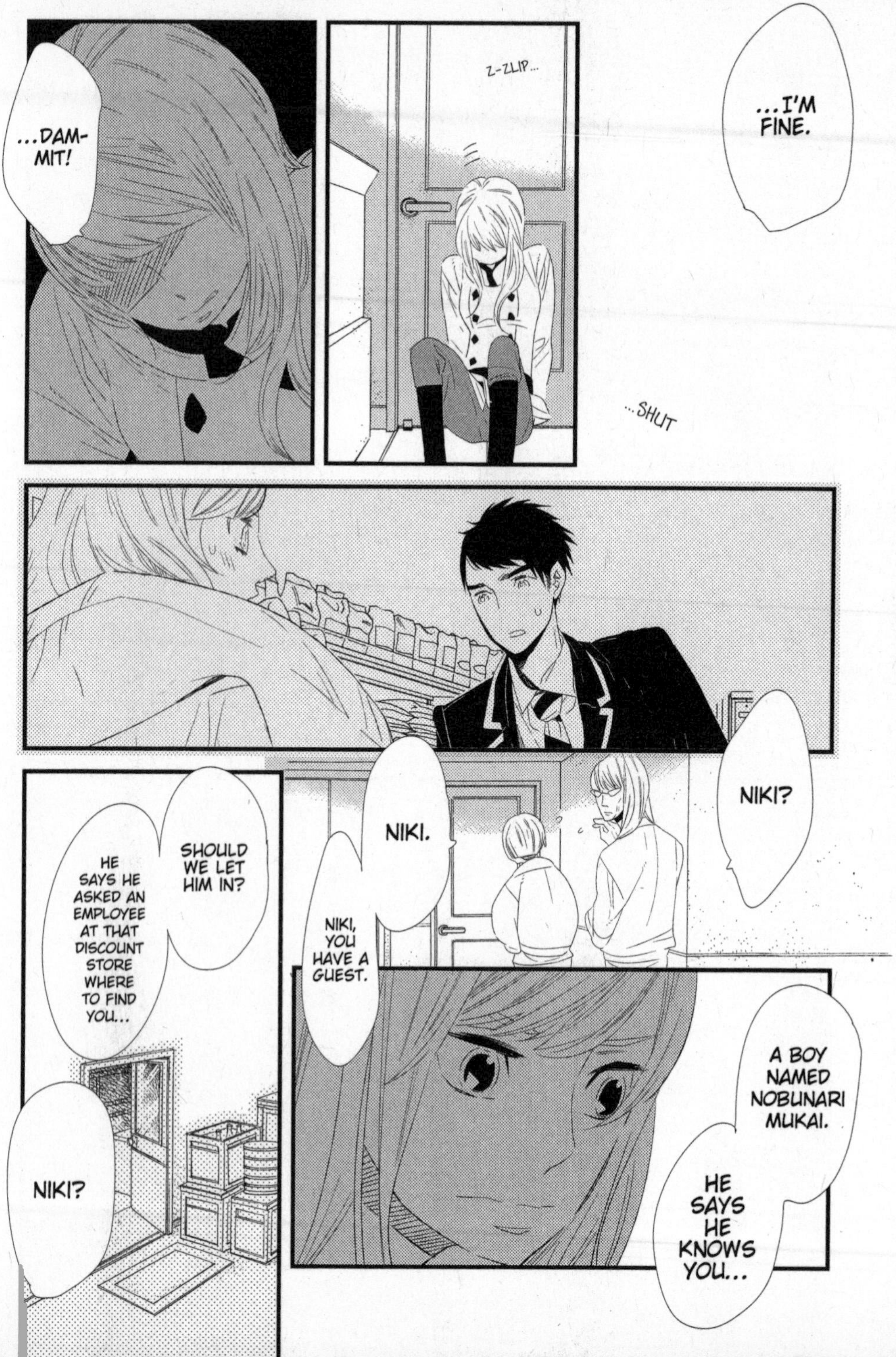
...I'M FINE.
...SHUT
Z-ZLIP...
...DAM-MIT!
NIKI?
NIKI.
NIKI, YOU HAVE A GUEST.
A BOY NAMED NOBUNARI MUKAI.
HE SAYS HE KNOWS YOU...
SHOULD WE LET HIM IN?
HE SAYS HE ASKED AN EMPLOYEE AT THAT DISCOUNT STORE WHERE TO FIND YOU...
NIKI?

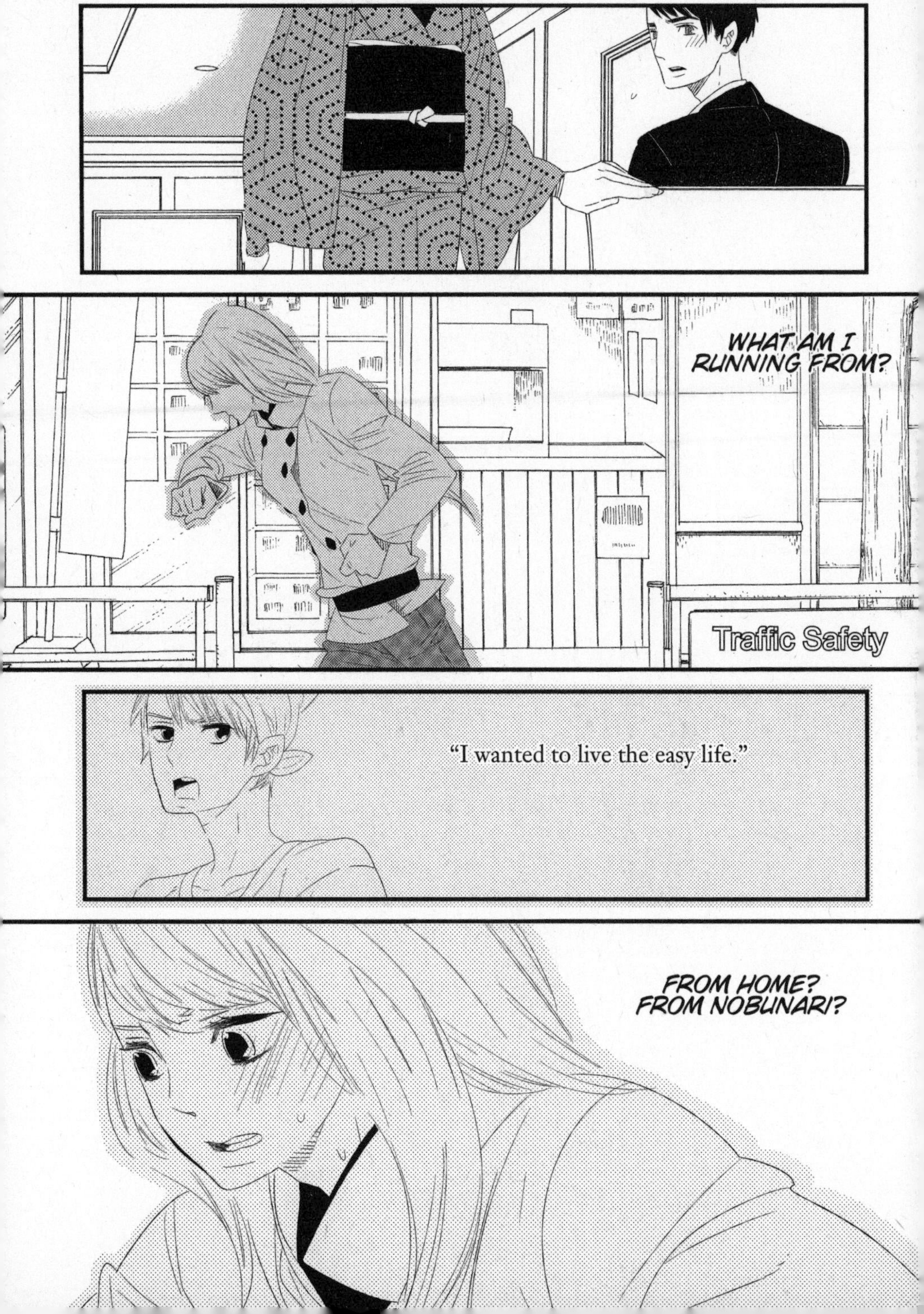
WHAT AM I
RUNNING FROM?
Traffic Safety
"I wanted to live the easy life."
FROM HOME?
FROM NOBUNARI?

AND YOU CAN NEVER HIDE IT, NOT EVEN IF YOU USE BOTH HANDS.

"You..."

"...will never know how I feel, Itaru!!"

YES!! HE HAD AN ADAM'S APPLE!

YOU *SURE* SHE'S A DUDE?

I TRIED!

UGH, WHY DIDN'T YOU STOP ME SOONER?!

THEN DO AS I TELL YOU!!

BECAUSE... I'M YOUR MANSERVANT.

GO HOME!

WHY WOULD I?! AND WHAT ABOUT *YOU*, ITARU-SAN?! WHY WON'T *YOU* GO HOME?!

WHY NOT?!

HMPH

NO. I DON'T WANT TO.

...WHAT?!

You're right!

LOOK AT YOUR ROUGH SKIN! YOU'VE BEEN USING CHEAP SOAP, HAVEN'T YOU?!

NO, IT IS NOT!

'CAUSE THIS IS MORE MY STYLE!!

Come on, let's go.

...SQUEEZE

DO YOU...

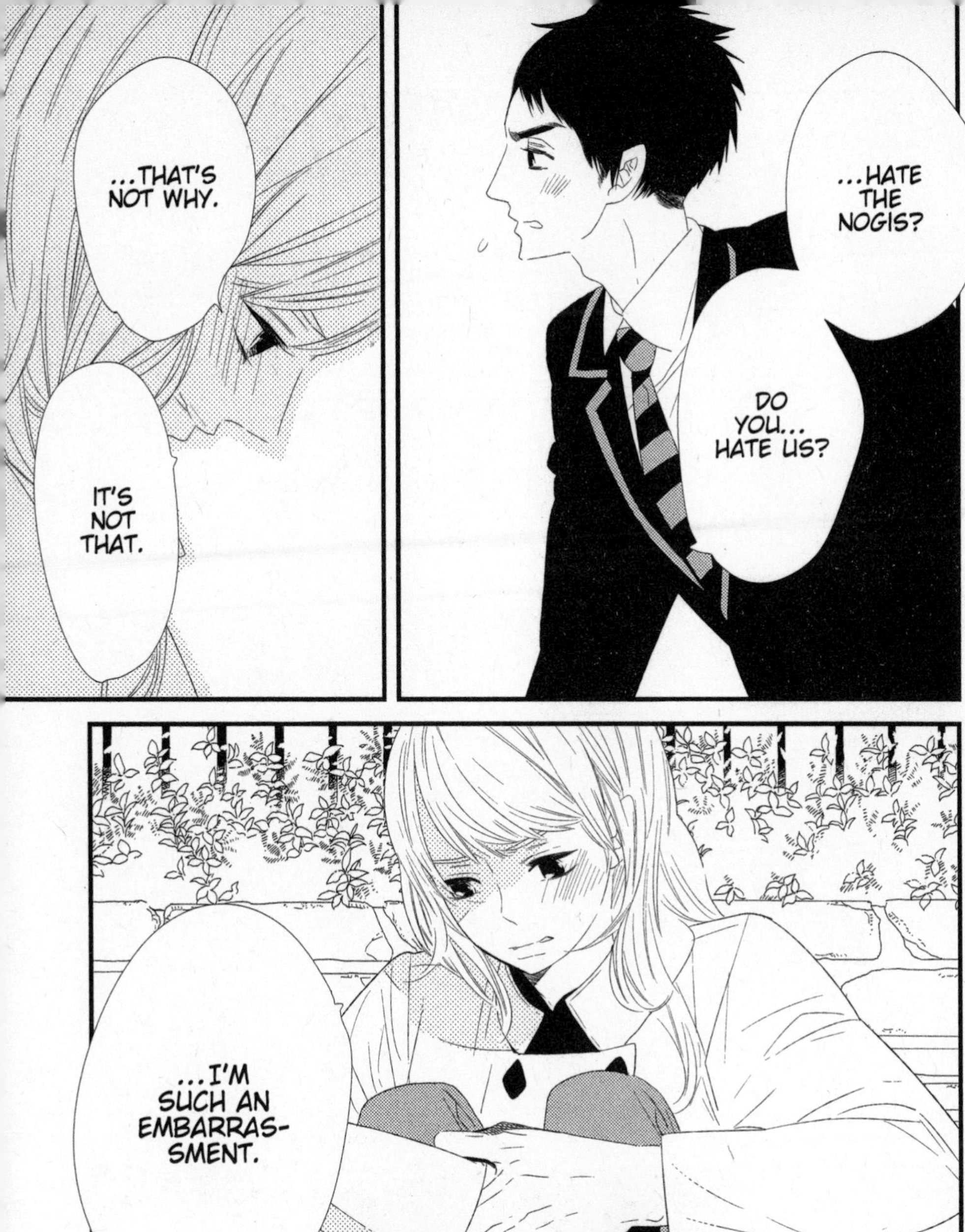
...HATE THE NOGIS?
DO YOU... HATE US?
...THAT'S NOT WHY.
IT'S NOT THAT.
...I'M SUCH AN EMBARRAS-SMENT.

...very good care of yourself.

...

...WHAT?!

HERE.

IT'S JUST A BLISTER.

YEAH, I'M FINE.

...IS YOUR FOOT ALL RIGHT?

HOBBLE

chapter
8

A CHARITY PARTY?

YOU WANT *ME* TO GO? TO *A PARTY*?

Ngh...
MONEY FOR EDUCATION...

THAT'S JUST A FRONT, THOUGH. THE TRUTH IS, ANZAI IS A MEDIA MOGUL AND HIS WIFE LOVES PARTIES.

STICKING THE WORD "CHARITY" ON IT MAKES FOR A BETTER PUBLIC IMAGE.

THEN I'M *NOT* GOING!

Give it back!

What is this?

Give it back!

YES. IT'S AN ANNUAL FUNCTION HELD TO RAISE MONEY FOR THE EDUCATION OF CHILDREN WHO HAVE LOST THEIR PARENTS IN TRAFFIC ACCIDENTS.

Yeah, but...
I BET I'LL HAVE TO PUT ON MENSWEAR AND DANCE AS A MAN!

WHY NOT? YOU'LL GET TO DRESS UP AND GO DANCING.

NO, I'M NOT!

YOU'RE GOING.

OF COURSE YOU WILL.

98

YES. ANYTHING WITHIN THE POWER OF MY FINANCES.

OKAY... I'LL DO IT!

WHAT'S SHE GONNA WISH FOR?

CLOTHES? A RAISE?

SHE AGREED TO THAT SURPRISINGLY EASILY.

...GOOD. THEN LET'S START YOUR LESSON.

SHUT...

SQUEAK...

SQUEAK...

100

THIS IS GOING TO BE A BATTLE OF STRENGTH.

HNGH

HNGH

Poultry for building muscles.

PLEASE DO KEEP IN MIND...ALL THINGS IN MODERATION.

UM...

UM...

ATSUKO-SAN...ARE YOU *SURE* THAT PUTTING ON SO MUCH MUSCLE MASS WON'T CAUSE YOU PROBLEMS LATER?

I'll be fine. Burp.

GLUG

GLUG

GLUG

PHEW...

RISE... RISE...

LOWER...

...

BM TSS TSS

BM TSS TSS

I WAS HOPING THAT IT WOULD BE A MORE NATURAL FIT ON YOU LIKE THIS.

...SMILE

I USED THE SHAPING SUIT YOU MADE AS REFERENCE...

AND HAD ITARU-SAMA'S TUXEDO TAILORED TO YOUR MEASURE-MENTS.

AND THE SLEEVES AREN'T BAGGY.

OOOH...

IT'S A PERFECT FIT...

FLUTTER...

AND THIS IS FROM ME.

HERE. THESE SHOULD MAKE THINGS A BIT EASIER FOR YOU.

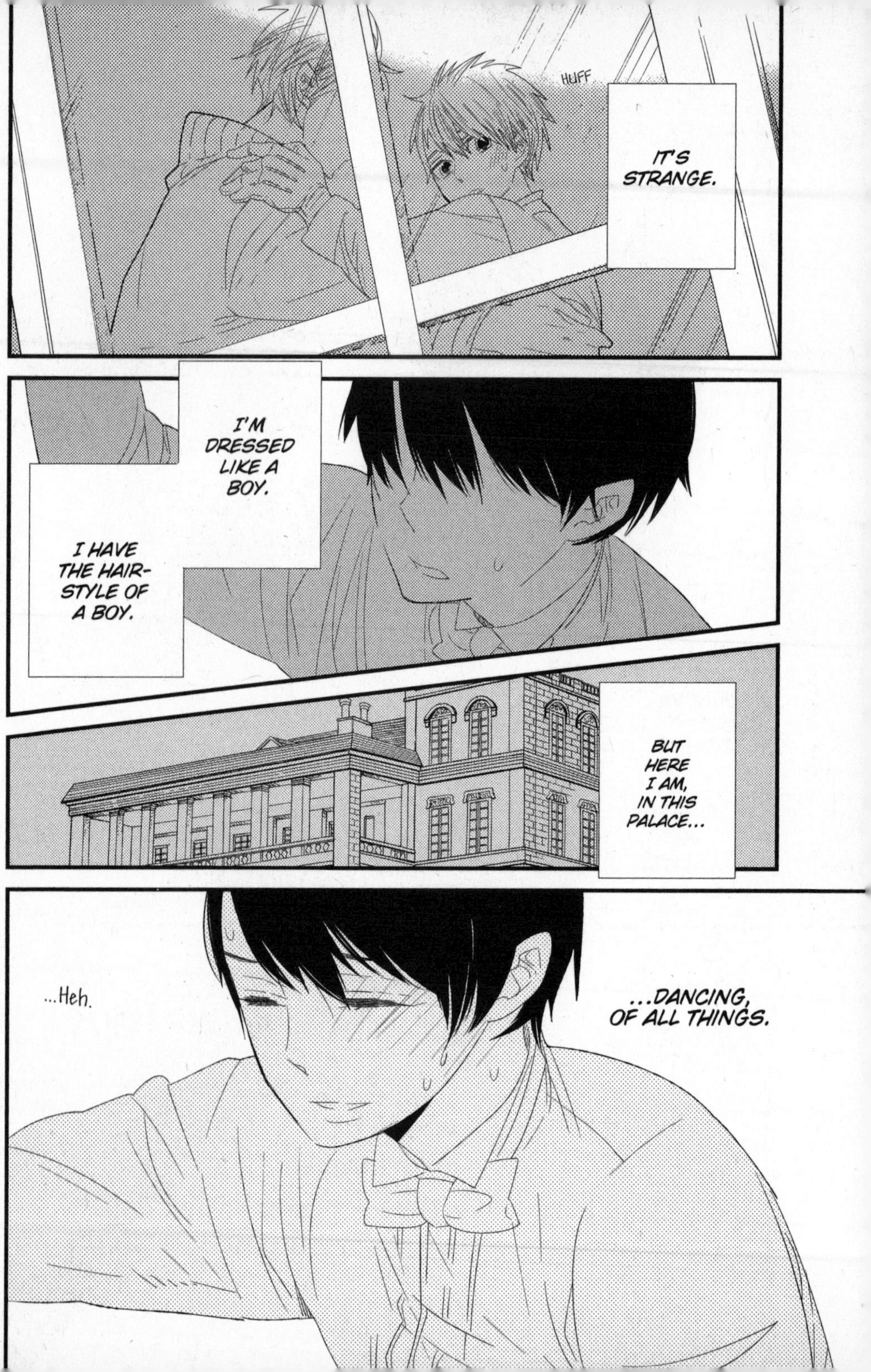
IT'S STRANGE.
HUFF
I'M DRESSED LIKE A BOY.
I HAVE THE HAIR-STYLE OF A BOY.
BUT HERE I AM, IN THIS PALACE...
...DANCING, OF ALL THINGS.
...Heh.

122

124

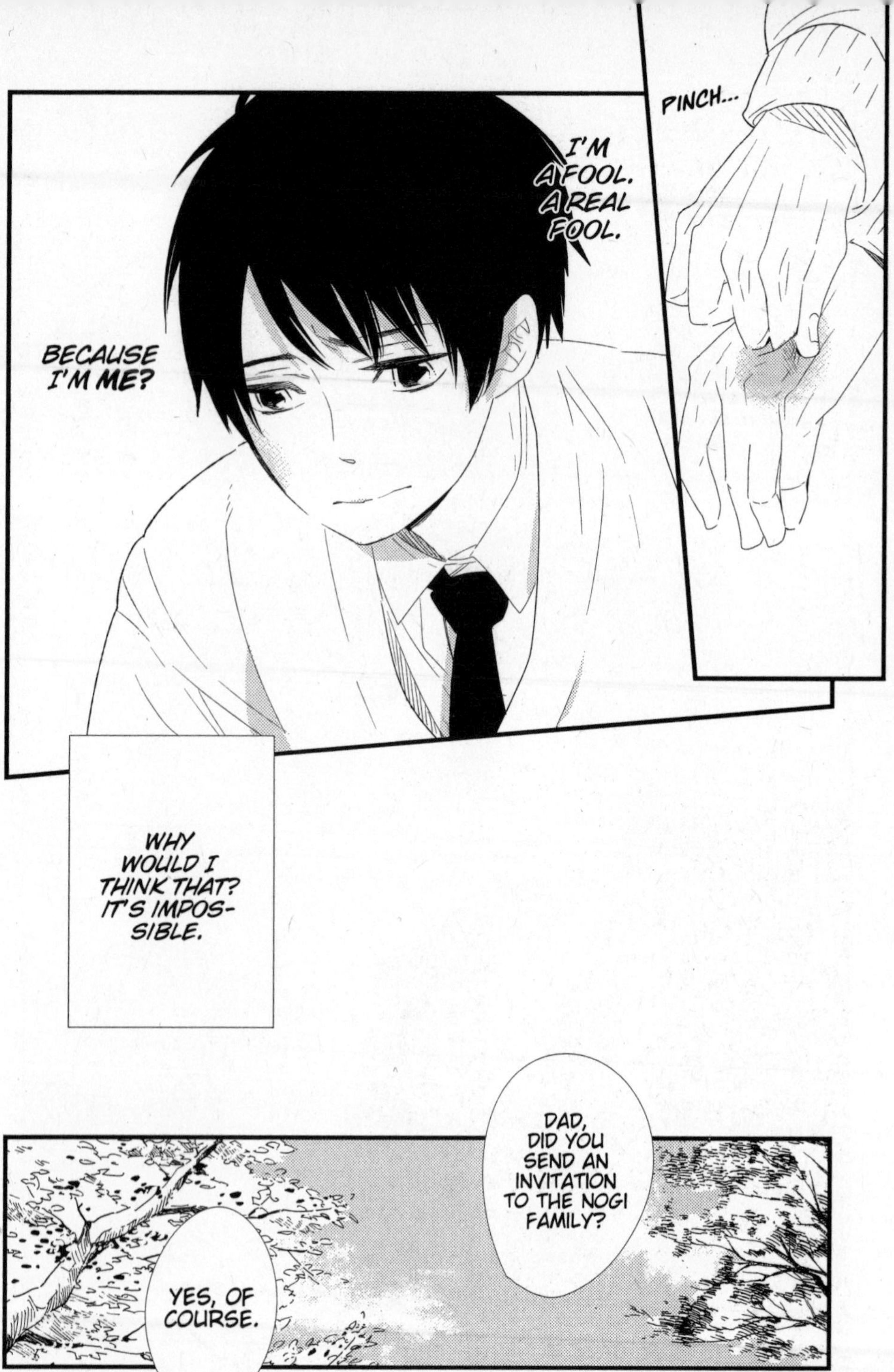
PINCH...
I'M A FOOL. A REAL FOOL.
BECAUSE I'M ME?
WHY WOULD I THINK THAT? IT'S IMPOSSIBLE.
DAD, DID YOU SEND AN INVITATION TO THE NOGI FAMILY?
YES, OF COURSE.

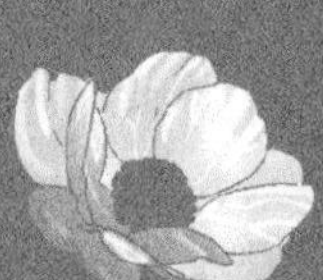

the prince in his dark days
hico yamanaka

chapter 9

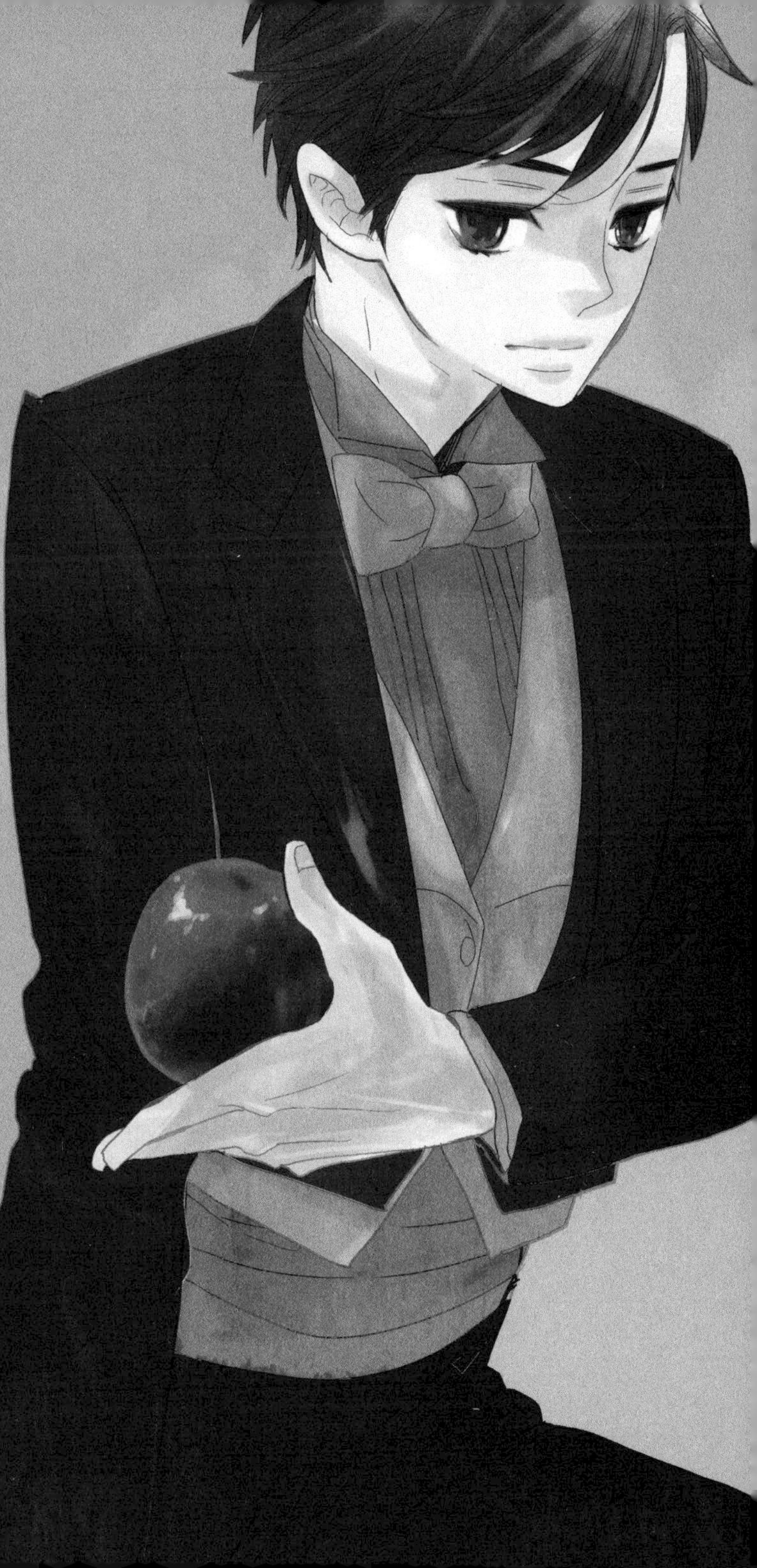

the prince in his dark days
Hico Yamanaka

THE ANZAI FAMILY STARTED AS A COMPUTER SOFTWARE FIRM, THEN RAPIDLY EXPANDED.

THEY BOUGHT UP TŌWA TV FIVE YEARS AGO, AND THERE ARE RUMORS OF THEM GETTING INTO POLITICS...

HMMM.

IN 1996, THEY TOOK THEIR COMPANY PUBLIC ON THE TOKYO STOCK EXCHANGE, AND AFTER THAT, THEY KEPT EXPANDING THROUGH DIVERSIFICATION, OVERSEAS MARKETING, ETC.

UH-HUH.

...

...

IS THERE SOMETHING YOU WANT TO SAY TO ME?

I'm just looking after her because she's his double.

...NOT REALLY.

IT'S NOT LIKE THAT WAS SHOCKING NEWS.

REALLY.

...I'M FINE.

THIS...THIS MANSION IS AMAZING...

I THINK IT'S AS BIG AS THE NOGI ESTATE.

THIS ONE AND THE NOGI ESTATE WERE BOTH BUILT ABOUT A HUNDRED YEARS AGO.

Well, if it isn't Hosokawa-sensei.

Thank you so much for joining us today!

So they let you out of Nagata, eh?

THE ANZAIS DIDN'T OWN IT UNTIL FIVE YEARS AGO.

DON'T COMPARE THE NOGIS TO NEW MONEY.

BUT THIS ONE HAS CHANGED OWNERS ABOUT FIVE TIMES ALREADY.

THAT'S DAIGO, THE ONLY SON OF THE ANZAI FAMILY. HE'S A FIRST-YEAR AT SHŪ ACADEMY HIGH SCHOOL, WHICH MAKES HIM OUR UNDERCLASSMAN.

WELCOME, AND THANK YOU FOR COMING.

PLEASE, LET ME ESCORT YOU TO THE BALLROOM.

HE'S ONLY A FRESHMAN, BUT HE'S ALREADY THE VICE PRESIDENT OF THE VOLUNTEERING CLUB, AND HE'S HELPING BY TAKING IN FOREIGN EXCHANGE STUDENTS. HE'S AN UNUSUAL TYPE IN OUR SCHOOL.

BUT ITARU *DOES* ATTEND THE ANZAIS' PARTY EVERY YEAR.

NO, NOT IN PARTICULAR.

IS HE CLOSE TO ITARU?

...SO THERE *ARE* RICH PEOPLE LIKE THAT.

DAZE...

HE IS WELL-MANNERED, AND SEEMS SO KIND.

Hyaaa ha ha ha!

Seize her!

Arrogant

Not every family in Japan...

...can afford knives and forks.

Snide

NOT LIKE ITARU... OR LIKE RYŌ, OR NOBU-NARI-SAN, EITHER.

135

WINCE

LIKE A CHARMING PRINCE.

...SMILE

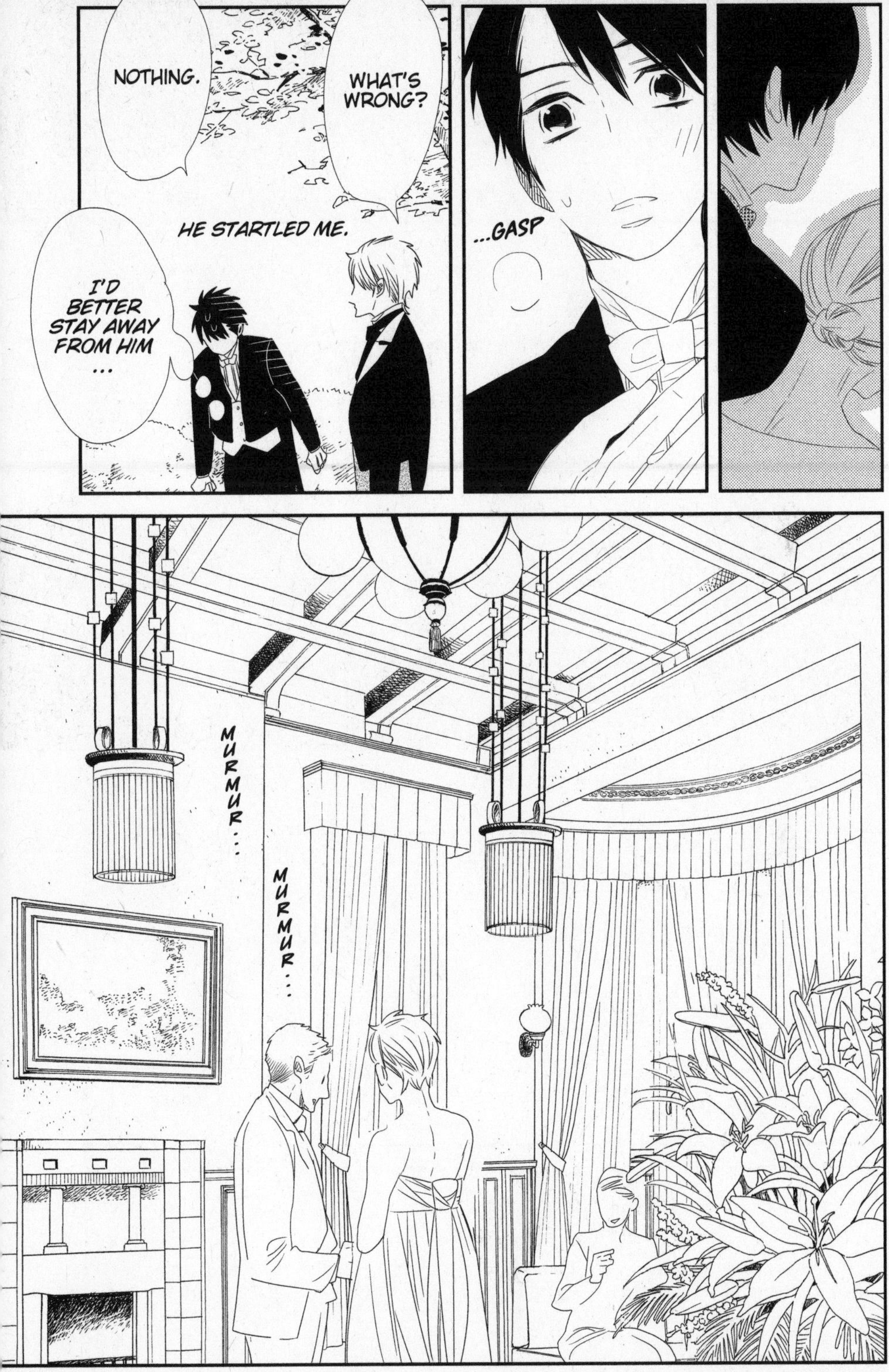
...GASP
WHAT'S WRONG?
NOTHING.
HE STARTLED ME.
I'D BETTER STAY AWAY FROM HIM ...
MURMUR...
MURMUR...

138

...AND SUFFOCATING.

HEY, YOU. AREN'T YOU GONNA DANCE?

ALL ALONE...

...

GNN...

THE ONLY SON OF THE NOGI FAMILY.

...DO WE KNOW EACH OTHER?

ARROGANT. SELF-IMPORTANT...

NO! BUT... EVERYONE KNOWS YOU.

I... ITARU-SAMA!! HOW... HOW DO YOU DO?

THE BABY-FACED RUFFIAN.

I... I KNOW THAT THESE CLOTHES WOULD NEVER SUIT A GIRL LIKE ME, BUT...!

IT'S PRE...

MY PARENTS INSISTED THAT I GO TO A PARTY.

THEY EVEN BOUGHT ME A DRESS!

You're the cutest girl in Japan!

You look lovely, Yōko-chan!

BLUSH

A BOY WHO LIVES IN A DIFFERENT WORLD.

THAT DRESS...

AND THEY DID BUY ME THE DRESS, SO...!

BUT MY PARENTS... THEY THINK I'M THEIR PERFECT LITTLE GIRL!

146

HUH?!

...!

SHUT UP!

...WHO SAID YOU COULD WATCH?!

TUG

Yeah! THAT WAS AWESOME! THAT'S OUR ITARU-SAMA!

WHAT! WHY YOU—!

...PROB-ABLY.

AND THERE ARE STILL A LOT OF ROOMS LIKE THIS ONE, THAT DON'T HAVE ANY FURNITURE.

...WE HAVEN'T LIVED HERE LONG.

I'M SURE YOUR MANSION IS FULL OF OLD THINGS YOU INHERITED FROM YOUR ANCESTORS.

WELL, YEAH.

BUT WE STILL HAVEN'T MANAGED TO FILL HALF OF THIS HOUSE.

CLATTER...

WE MOVED HERE FIVE YEARS AGO, AND WE'VE SPENT ALL KINDS OF MONEY ON ALL KINDS OF THINGS.

IT MAY LOOK LIKE A PALACE AT FIRST GLANCE, LIKE YOURS.

BUT YOUR HOUSE REALLY ISN'T LIKE MINE, ITARU-SENPAI.

Eh heh heh.

Don't compare it to the Nogis.

154

157

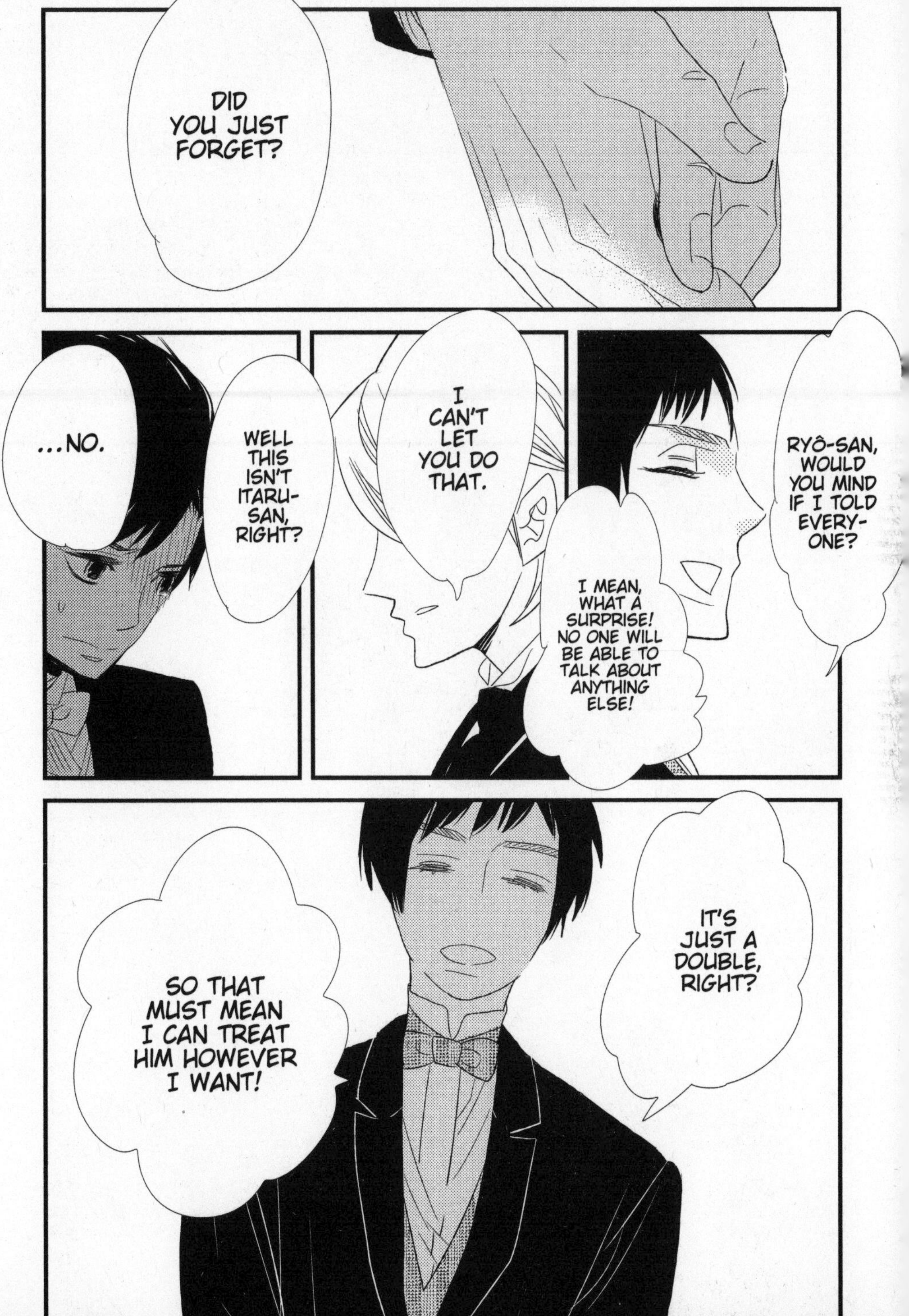
DID YOU JUST FORGET?
RYÔ-SAN, WOULD YOU MIND IF I TOLD EVERY-ONE?
I MEAN, WHAT A SURPRISE! NO ONE WILL BE ABLE TO TALK ABOUT ANYTHING ELSE!
I CAN'T LET YOU DO THAT.
WELL THIS ISN'T ITARU-SAN, RIGHT?
...NO.
IT'S JUST A DOUBLE, RIGHT?
SO THAT MUST MEAN I CAN TREAT HIM HOWEVER I WANT!

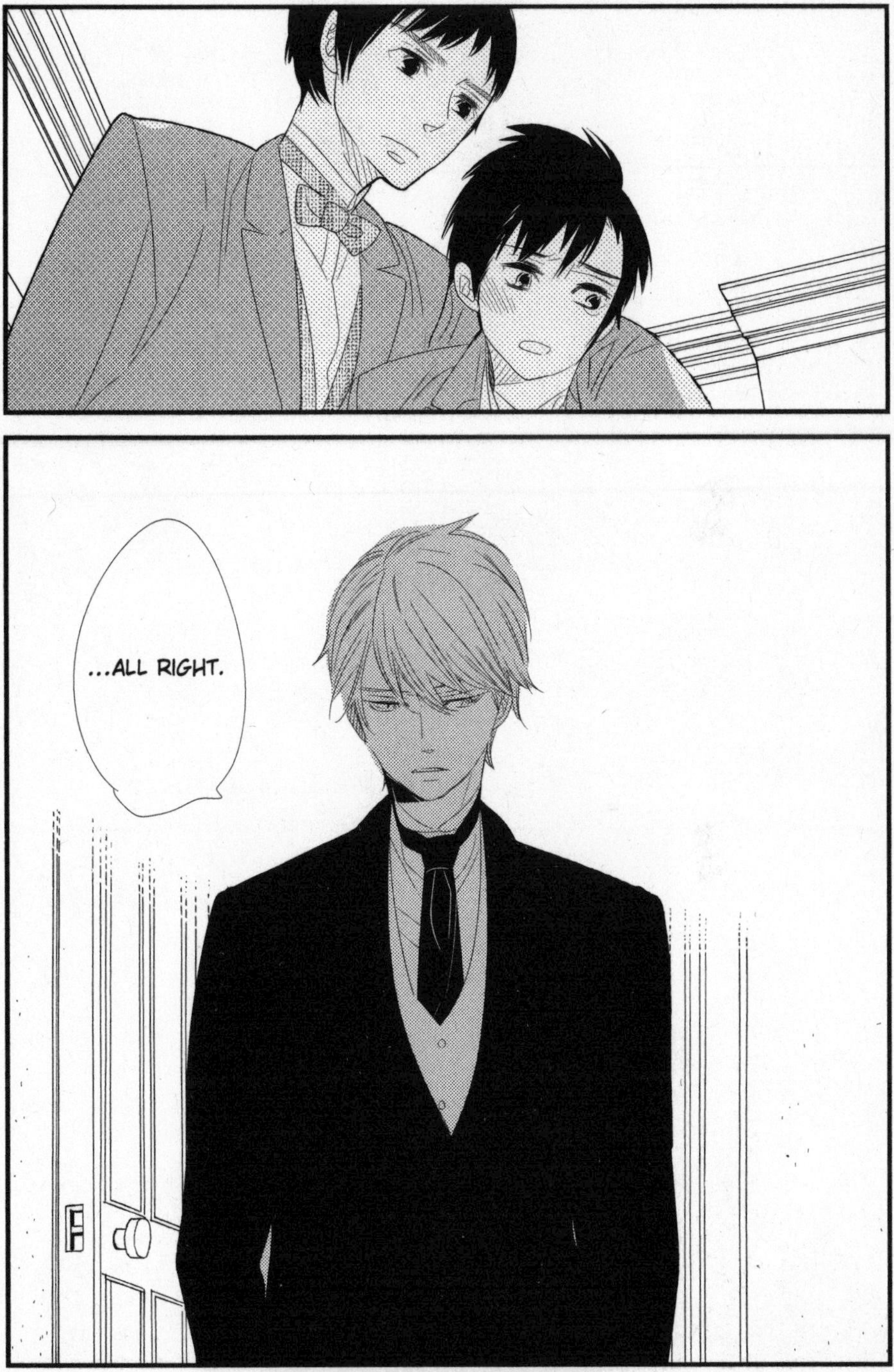
...ALL RIGHT.

to be continued in vol. 3

UNLIKE THEM, I HAVE THINGS TO DO.

GAH!

Wah! ITARU-SAN, ARE YOU ALL RIGHT?!

HUH?

...THAT'S OKAY.

I LIKE IT LIKE THIS.

WHAT ...?

I HAVE BANDAGES!

UGH...

Dammit!

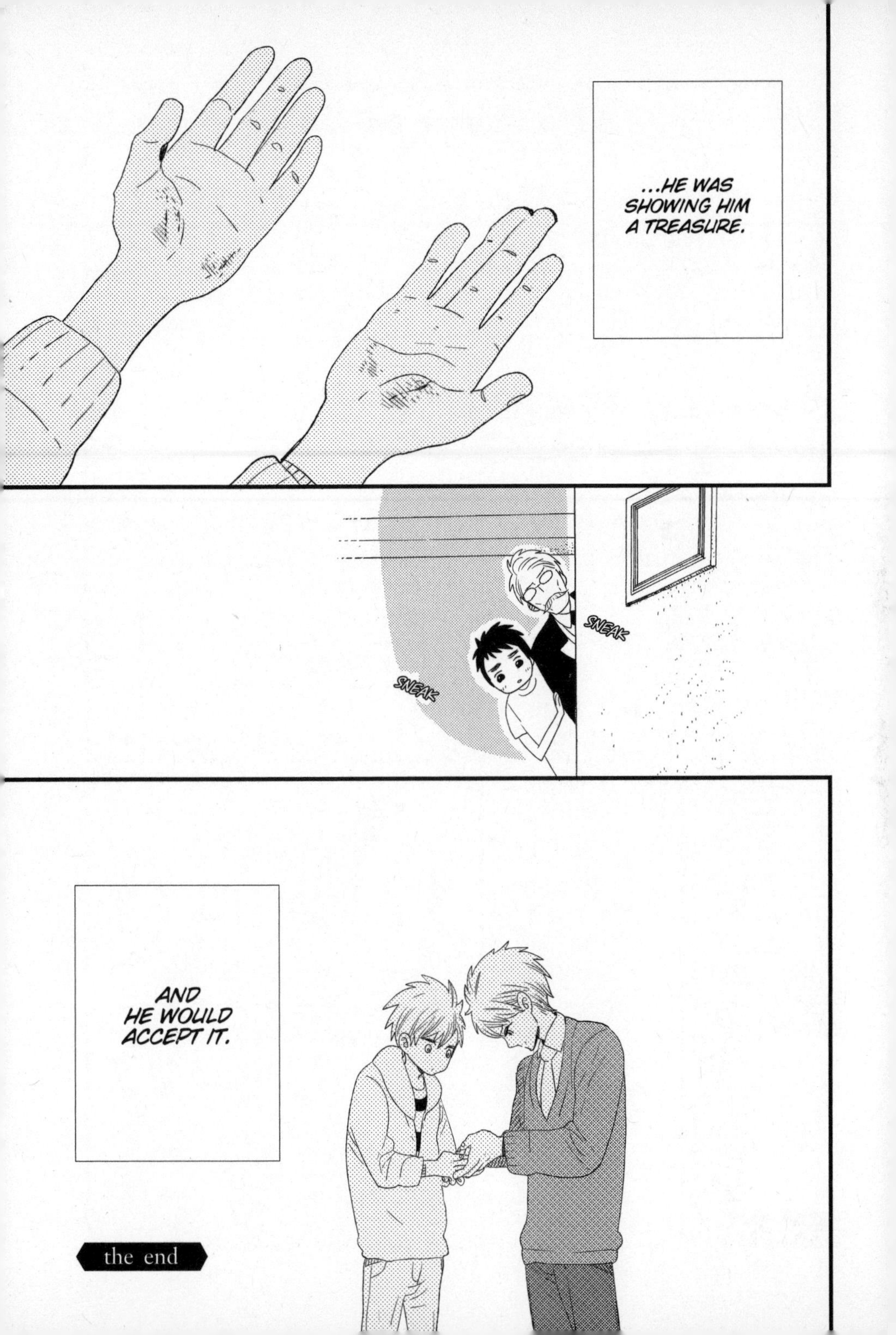
...HE WAS SHOWING HIM A TREASURE.
SNEAK
SNEAK
AND HE WOULD ACCEPT IT.
the end

Translation Notes

I'm a busy man, page 13

Here, Itaru uses the first-person pronoun ore, which is a typically masculine way to say "I." As a woman, it is considered rude and inappropriate to refer to the self as ore. A Japanese reader would have recognized the masculine speech pattern right away.

If it were a big bottle, page 28

In Japanese host bars and clubs like these, one can order a bottle that is put on hold for a specific patron. The patron can keep coming back to share a drink from the same bottle with their preferred host(s).

Nickie versus Niki, page 28

In the English pronunciation, Itaru's chosen name Nickie sounds like the shorter version, Niki. But in Japanese, the name has an extra syllable. When pronounced in Japanese, it sounds like "nick-key."

Drag princess, page 30

The term used here is Joso-ko. It is a made up nickname using the words josou, which means to "dress up as a woman" and -ko, which is a common ending for girl's names.

Sissy, page 40

In this panel, Itaru is called an okama, which is the most commonly used Japanese term referring to gay men. It is not always an insult, for many people self-identify as okama, too. The definition itself has changed throughout the years. For example, in the early 2000s, the term connoted more of a gendered performance, not just a specific sexuality or romantic interest. Since then, and today, okama has come to refer to people in male-to-male relationships more broadly. But in the context of two children fighting, calling someone an okama implies that they must be gay because they are males who are effeminate in personality, character, mannerisms, and speech.

Your face is small, page 73

This is commonly said in Japan of people with beautiful faces, but it doesn't necessarily have to do with the actual size of the face. Often it has more to do with proportions—either of the face itself, or of the face in relation to the body. Having a small face can be a delicate or dainty feature for a woman. It can also refer to having a cute, childlike face.

Bunmeido dorayaki, page 79

Bunmeido is a famous Japanese store that specializes in sweets. Dorayaki is a popular Japanese sweet snack made of two fluffy, circular cakes, with red bean paste in the middle.

That discount store, page 82

Although the original Japanese text erased part of the words, enough of it is left to tell Japanese readers that the thrift store in question is Don Quijote. This chain sells a variety of goods, including groceries.

Dosukoi, page 142

Dosukoi is derived from *dokkoi*, an interjection used when doing heavy labor (something like an "oof!"). This specific pronunciation of *dosukoi* is yelled by sumo wrestlers during a match.

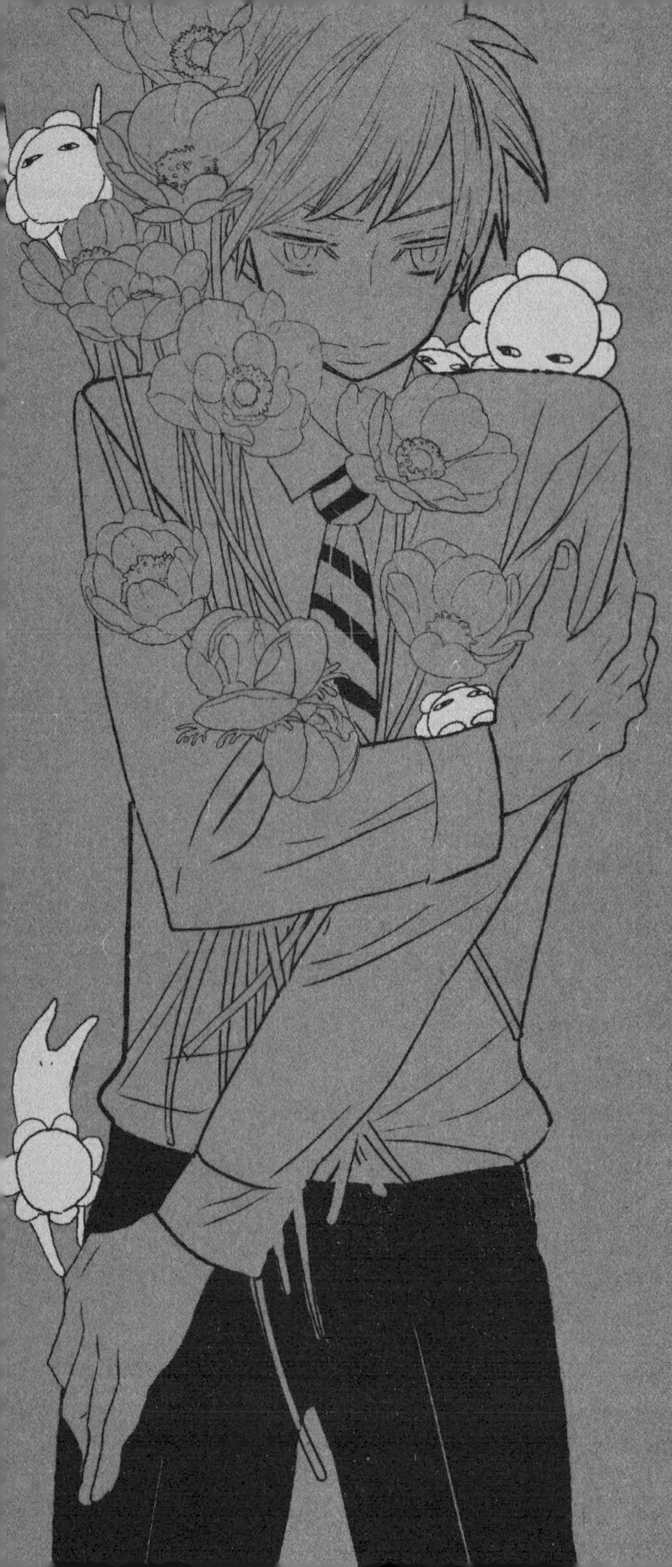

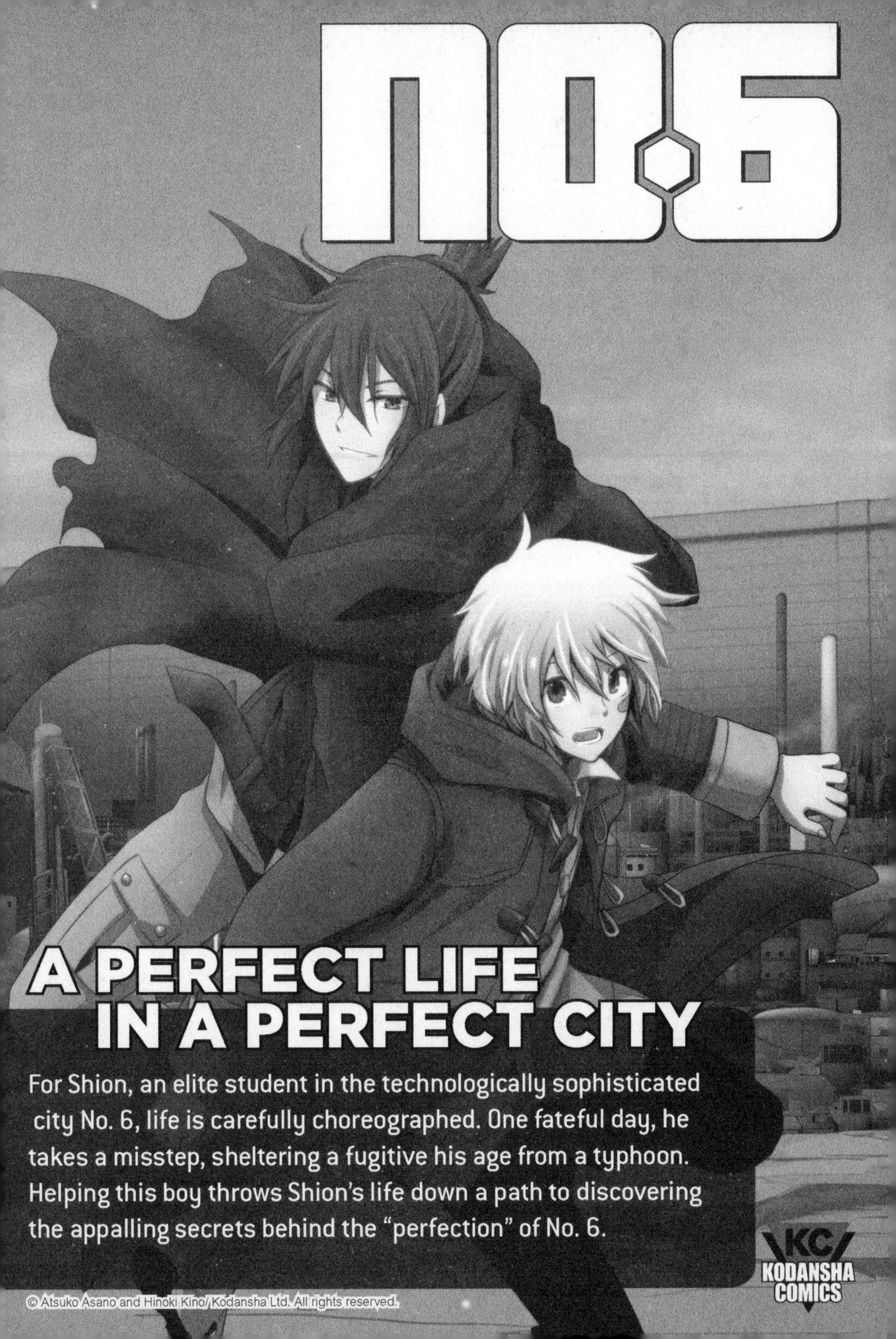
NO.6
A PERFECT LIFE
IN A PERFECT CITY
For Shion, an elite student in the technologically sophisticated city No. 6, life is carefully choreographed. One fateful day, he takes a misstep, sheltering a fugitive his age from a typhoon. Helping this boy throws Shion's life down a path to discovering the appalling secrets behind the "perfection" of No. 6.
KC
KODANSHA
COMICS
© Atsuko Asano and Hinoki Kino/ Kodansha Ltd. All rights reserved.

Praise for the anime:

"The show provides a pleasant window on the highs and lows of young love with two young people who are first timers at the real thing."

-The Fandom Post

"Always it is smarter, more poetic, more touching, just plain better than you think it is going to be."

-Anime News Network

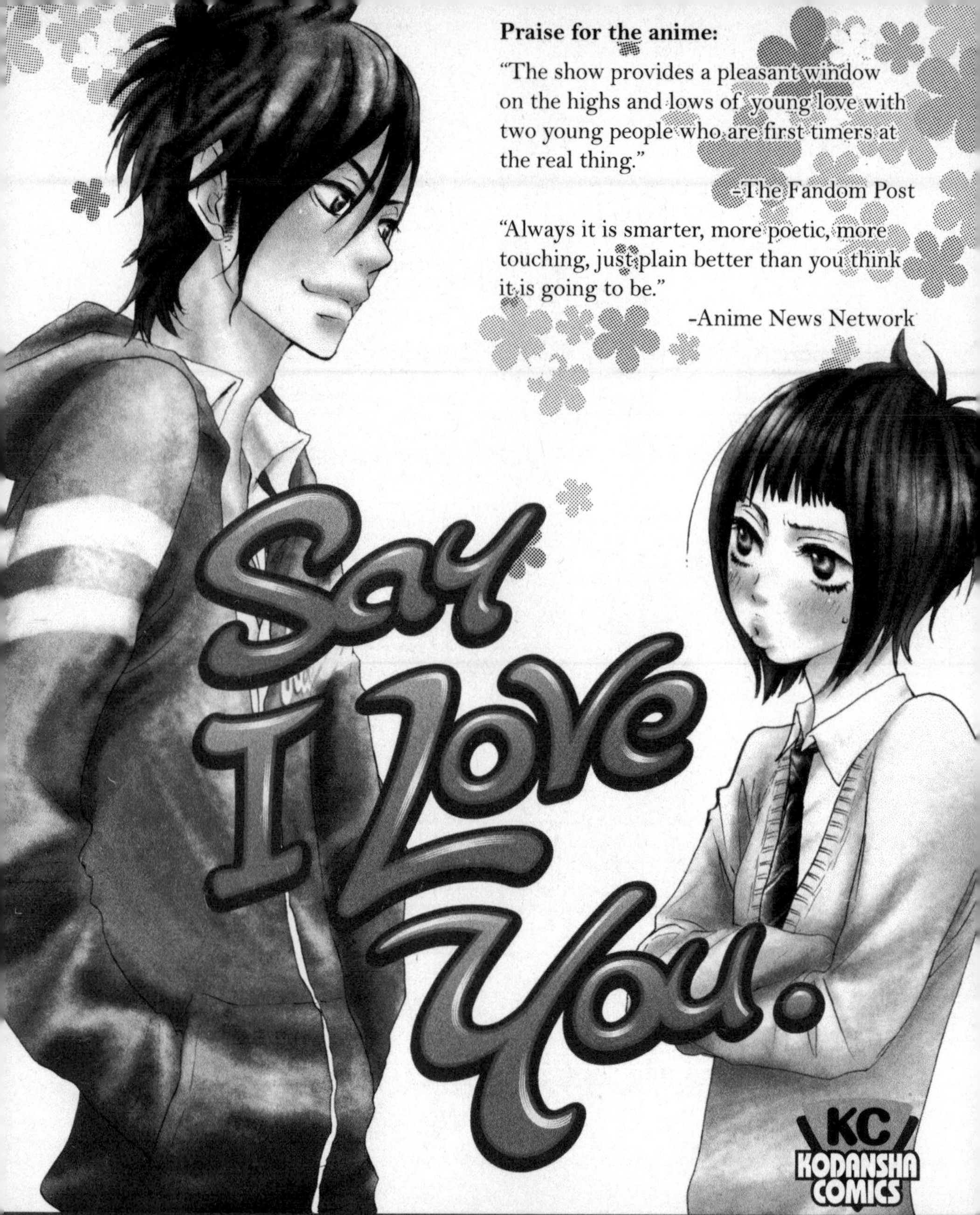
Say I Love You.
KC
KODANSHA COMICS

Mei Tachibana has no friends — and says she doesn't need them!

But everything changes when she accidentally roundhouse kicks the most popular boy in school! However, Yamato Kurosawa isn't angry in the slightest—in fact, he thinks his ordinary life could use an unusual girl like Mei. But winning Mei's trust will be a tough task. How long will she refuse to say, "I love you"?

A Silent Voice

"The word heartwarming was made for manga like this."
–Manga Bookshelf

"A harsh and biting social commentary... delivers in its depth of character and emotional strength." -Comics Bulletin

"A very powerful story about being different and the consequences of childhood bullying... Read it."
–Anime News Network

Shoya is a bully. When Shoko, a girl who can't hear, enters his elementary school class, she becomes their favorite target, and Shoya and his friends goad each other into devising new tortures for her. But the children's cruelty goes too far. Shoko is forced to leave the school, and Shoya ends up shouldering all the blame. Six years later, the two meet again. Can Shoya make up for his past mistakes, or is it too late?

Available now in print and digitally!

Maria
THE VIRGIN WITCH

PURITY AND POWER

As a war to determine the rightful ruler of medieval France ravages the land, the witch Maria decides she will not stand idly by as men kill each other in the name of God and glory. Using her powerful magic, she summons various beasts and demons —even going as far as using a succubus to seduce soldiers into submission under the veil of night— all to stop the needless slaughter. However, after the Archangel Michael puts an end to her meddling, he curses her to lose her powers if she ever gives up her virginity. Will she forgo the forbidden fruit of adulthood in order to bring an end to the merciless machine of war?
Available now in print and digitally!

Yamada-kun AND THE Seven Witches

"A very funny manga with a lot of heart and character."
—Adventures in Poor Taste

SWAPPED WITH A KISS?!

Class troublemaker Ryu Yamada is already having a bad day when he stumbles down a staircase along with star student Urara Shiraishi. When he wakes up, he realizes they have switched bodies—and that Ryu has the power to trade places with anyone just by kissing them! Ryu and Urara take full advantage of the situation to improve their lives, but with such an oddly amazing power, just how long will they be able to keep their secret under wraps?

Available now in print and digitally!

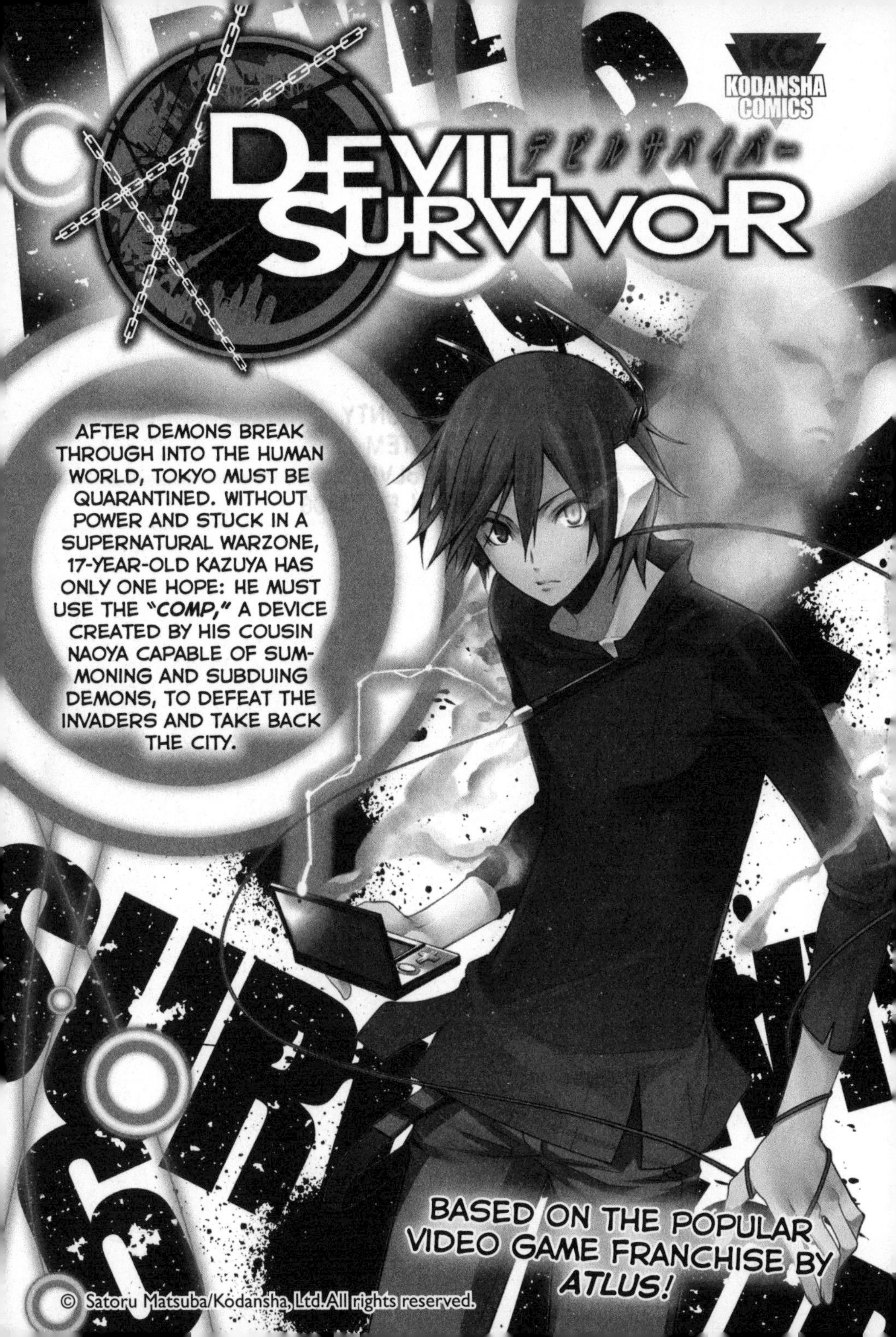
KODANSHA COMICS
DEVIL SURVIVOR
デビルサバイバー
AFTER DEMONS BREAK THROUGH INTO THE HUMAN WORLD, TOKYO MUST BE QUARANTINED. WITHOUT POWER AND STUCK IN A SUPERNATURAL WARZONE, 17-YEAR-OLD KAZUYA HAS ONLY ONE HOPE: HE MUST USE THE "COMP," A DEVICE CREATED BY HIS COUSIN NAOYA CAPABLE OF SUMMONING AND SUBDUING DEMONS, TO DEFEAT THE INVADERS AND TAKE BACK THE CITY.
BASED ON THE POPULAR VIDEO GAME FRANCHISE BY ATLUS!
© Satoru Matsuba/Kodansha, Ltd. All rights reserved.

The Prince in His Dark Days volume 2 is a work of fiction. Names, characters, places, and incidents are the products of the author's imagination or are used fictitiously. Any resemblance to actual events, locales, or persons, living or dead, is entirely coincidental.

A Kodansha Comics Trade Paperback Original
The Prince in His Dark Days volume 2 copyright © 2012 Hico Yamanaka
English translation copyright © 2016 Hico Yamanaka

Published in the United States by Kodansha Comics, an imprint of
Kodansha USA Publishing, LLC, New York.

Publication rights for this English edition arranged through
Kodansha Ltd, Tokyo.

ISBN 978-1-63236-368-8

Printed in the United States of America.

www.kodanshacomics.com

9 8 7 6 5 4 3 2 1
Translation: Alethea and Athena Nibley
Lettering: Maggie Vicknair
Editing: Haruko Hashimoto
Kodansha Comics edition cover design by Phil Balsman